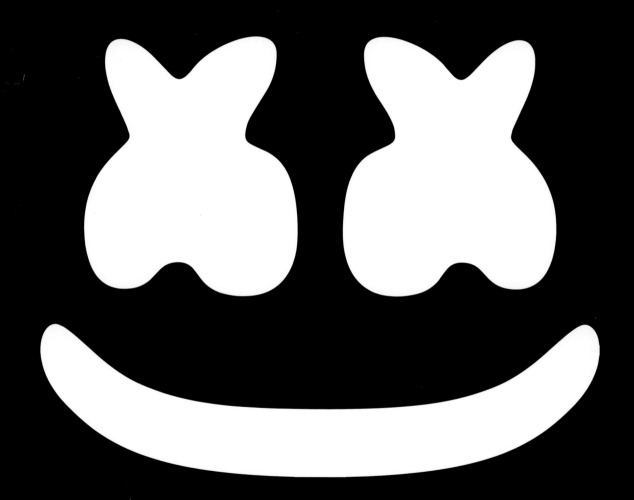

COOKING WITH MARSHMELLO

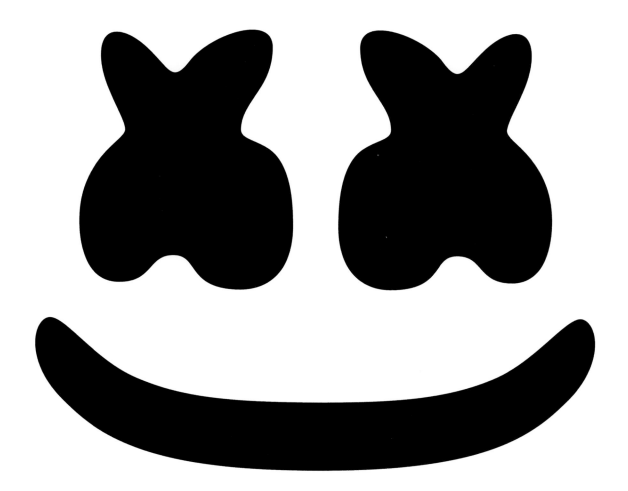

RECIPES WITH A REMIX

Publisher Mike Sanders
Art Director William Thomas
Editorial Director Ann Barton
Senior Designer Rebecca Batchelor
Senior Editor Olivia Peluso
Principal Photographer Noah Fecks
Proofreaders Rick Ball, Claire Safran
Indexer Johnna VanHoose Dinse

First American Edition, 2023
Published in the United States by DK Publishing
1745 Broadway, 20th Floor, New York, NY 10019

The authorized representative in the EEA is Dorling Kindersley
Verlag GmbH. Arnulfstr. 124, 80636 Munich, Germany

Library of Congress Catalog Number: 2023931637
ISBN 978-0-7440-8403-0

DK books are available at special discounts when purchased
in bulk for sales promotions, premiums, fundraising, or
educational use. For details, contact SpecialSales@dk.com

Printed and bound in China

Photo credits: page 11 © Gabe Tiano
pages 8, 20, 54, 88, 122, 156 © Stefan Ferra
pages 36–37, 72–73, 174–175 © Lance Skundrich

All other images © 2023 by Noah Fecks

For the curious
www.dk.com

TO THE MELLOGANG
NONE OF THIS WOULD BE POSSIBLE WITHOUT YOU!

CONTENTS

INTRODUCTION

COOKING WITH MARSHMELLO

In the same way that music brings people together around a common love, I've found that food is an equally powerful way for me to bridge the cultural gaps between my fans and people all over the world. When I reflect on the most important moments of my own life, so many of them involve music and food together. Some of my favorite memories consist of experiencing new dishes and flavors while on tour, or even just hanging out in the studio with friends discussing things that they need to try.

With all of the knowledge I gained, I really wanted to express my passion for cooking with Cooking with Marshmello on Youtube, Facebook, Tiktok, and Instagram, but this is my first actual cookbook, and I could not be more excited for your take on it.

I highly suggest that you approach some of these recipes the same way that I approach my music: with an open and creative mind. Dont ever be afraid to put your own spin on it. So dive into these pages and discover some of my favorite dishes. Let's get cooking!

ONE THING RIGHT

The key to cooking, whether you're a professional or amateur, is nailing the ground rules of the kitchen. Even if you just get one thing right, you'll be on your way to nailing it every time!

MAKING THE CUT

It seems backwards, but a sharp knife is a safe knife. Using a dull knife is dangerous, because you're putting yourself at risk for slips and accidents. A handheld knife sharpener is cheap to buy and easy to use, so make sure your knife set is always on point.

HOW TO SHARPEN YOUR KNIFE

THE MELLO WAY

Don't want to invest in a sharpener? Use a coffee mug instead! Flip it over so the rough, unglazed rim is pointing up and set the mug on a kitchen towel so it doesn't slip around. Hold the mug handle with one hand and the knife in your other hand. Aim for a 15° angle and drag the knife from base to tip along the rim closest to you. Repeat about 10 times, then flip the knife to sharpen again on the other side. Wash and dry before using!

GET A GRIP

Before you start slicing and dicing, make sure you have a firm grip on your knife. For beginner cooks, grab the handle tightly in your fist, making sure all your fingers are tucked behind the blade. Once you've gotten comfortable using your knife, give the blade grip a try. Pinch the top of the knife blade between your thumb and index finger, then wrap your middle, ring, and pinkie fingers around the handle. This gives you a lot more control and flexibility when cutting.

Once your knife hand is secure, check that your helping hand is equally safe! Make sure your food is lying flat on a secure surface, then make a claw with your hand. Set the claw firmly on the food, tucking the tips of your fingers slightly back and your knuckles slightly forward. As you're cutting, let your knuckles guide the knife as you move the claw along the food.

HOW TO DICE AN ONION WITH THE RIGHT GRIP

ACROSS THE BOARD

Cutting boards seem so sweet and innocent, but they're sneaky little things. Because lots of things pass over the surface, they can be a war zone of bacteria. Make sure you thoroughly wash and dry your cutting board when switching between raw meats and vegetables. Or invest in a set and keep separate boards for different ingredients.

They're also a danger zone for knife accidents. Make sure your board is secure and lying flat on a work surface. Clear away any clutter so you have plenty of room to work. A wobbly, slippery board is going to take your focus away from your knife, and we don't want any slip ups!

THE MELLO WAY

Fold two layers of paper towels on top of each other. Run under water and wring out so they're damp, but not wet. Lay the paper towel stack flat on your work surface and set your cutting board on top. The paper towels will keep the board secure and in place while you're working!

KILL IT WITH A SKILLET

The number one rule with skillet success is letting it preheat, just like you would with an oven. Set it on the burner (check the recipe for the temp). If you're adding oil, let it warm up until it's shimmering and sliding around the surface.

When you add ingredients, make sure you're leaving room and not crowding the skillet. (Work in batches if you have to!) A little room will let air flow and moisture evaporate so your food gets brown and crisp instead of steamy and wet.

WHIP IT UP

Recipes will tell you to stir, fold, or whip. Here's the right tool and technique for all three.

Stirring is the most basic task. Just grab a wooden spoon and get to work. But before you stir, make sure your bowl is larger than you need so you have plenty of room to mix.

Folding means combining ingredients gently, like thick batter and fluffy egg whites. Grab a rubber spatula and, with a light touch, run it across the bottom and up the side of the mixing bowl to fold the mixture over itself. Rotate the bowl after each fold to get an even mixture.

Whipping means rapidly stirring to blend or add lots of air to a mixture. Grab a whisk and hold it at a 45° angle. Keep your arm still and spin your wrist in a circle quickly to whip the ingredients. Tilting the bowl slightly is sometimes helpful to get everything even.

HOW TO STIR, FOLD, AND WHIP

THE MELLO WAY

Roll a kitchen towel into a long rope, then twist it into a circle. Set your mixing bowl in the center to keep it secure while you stir, fold, or whip.

GET READY, GET SET

Before you do anything, read the recipe from start to finish. Then read it again! Think of cooking as a journey. It's important to know where you're going before you start.

Now it's time to prep. Get all your ingredients together, measure them out, do any chopping or slicing, and line them up so you can work in order. When the heat is on, future you will be happy current you set them up for success.

COME TO YOUR SENSES

Use all your senses. Cooking is about timing, but it's also about intuition. Don't rush to the next step just because the recipe says 5 minutes and it's been 5 minutes. Use your eyes, ears, and nose to check that you're on track, and adjust your timing (or temperature) as needed.

The most important sense is taste. Every step of the way, take a little taste. Make sure your seasoning is on point, adding whatever you need to make the most delicious dish possible. It's the best way to learn and grow as a cook!

KEEP CALM AND COOK ON

Chill out. Knowing what you're doing leads to working with confidence. A confident cook is a happy cook. And a happy cook means the kitchen is a place for fun and celebration. That's what this book is really all about: recipes that celebrate food, flavor, and everything delicious in life.

Music is always a part of my life, even when I'm rolling up my sleeves to get cooking. So throw on this playlist, turn up the volume, and have a blast. Happy cooking!

COOKING WITH MARSHMELLO PLAYLIST

TOOLS OF THE TRADE

Before jumping into the kitchen, make sure you have what you need for success.

MELLO'S TOP 10 EQUIPMENT COUNTDOWN

10. Hot Spot: Get a thick set of **oven mitts** to keep your human mitts safe. Also grab a sturdy **trivet** for putting hot pots and pans down without ruining your surface.

9. Stir Things Up: A **strong whisk, wooden spoon, rubber spatula,** and **silicone tongs** will help you whip, stir, fold, and flip your way to perfection. (See page 13 for a guide to all things mixing.)

8. Flash in the Pan: A few simple **baking pans** will cover your bases. A 9 x 13-inch (23 x 33cm) rectangular pan, an 8-inch (20cm) square baking pan, a Bundt pan, and a 12-cup muffin pan are the perfect starter set for all things sweet and savory.

7. Feeling Electric: A good **high-speed blender** will help mix drinks, smoothie bowls, and batters with ease. A handheld electric mixer will get egg whites fluffy, cream whipped, and even shred chicken without breaking a sweat.

6. Super Base: Investing in a big, sturdy **cutting board** will give you plenty of room to work. If you have a wooden cutting board, always dry it standing up so the wood doesn't warp into a wobbly board. (A quick guide to board safety is on page 13.)

5. Mix It Up: Find a stackable set of small, medium, and large **mixing bowls** for easy storage and lots of options. Stainless steel is the best for easy cleaning and won't hold odors like plastic can.

4. Home Sheet Home: Find a couple of **rimmed baking sheets,** also known as half sheet pans, that's roughly 18 x 13 inches (46 x 33 cm) with a 1-inch (2.5cm) rim. They're a cook's best friend!

3. Put a Lid on It: Invest in large, medium, and small **saucepans** with lids. They're the workhorses of the stovetop.

2. Kill It with a Skillet: A **12-inch (30cm) nonstick skillet** will get you through almost everything with ease. (More on that on page 13.) Just don't invest a lot of money—unlike stainless steel, nonstick skillets only last a few years and should be replaced as soon as the coating starts to wear off.

1. Slice and Dice: An **8-inch (20cm) chef's knife** is the most important tool in the kitchen. Don't break the bank, find something in your budget. Just make sure it's comfortable, because you'll be using it a lot! Other useful knives to have on hand are a large serrated knife—great for cutting through crusty bread, peeling tough fruits like pineapples, or even slicing delicate tomatoes—and a small paring knife for small slices and precise trimming.

AIR FRYER 101

My favorite kitchen tool (and probably the one I use the most) is the air fryer. I love it so much, I even made my own line of fryers with CRUX!

An air fryer is basically a mini countertop oven that uses a fan to move hot air around, getting food brown and crispy at lightning speed. It's easier than deep frying and faster than waiting for an oven to preheat, so it's my go-to for everything from zapping frozen food to roasting vegetables, reheating leftovers to cooking meat.

You'll see the air fryer pop up all over this book—for everything from snacks to desserts. There are a few key rules for air fryer success.

1 **Don't crowd the basket.** Work in batches if you have to, so everything has plenty of room to cook.

2 **Check often.** All the recipes in this book have temperatures and timings, but each brand of air fryer works differently, so pull out the basket and take a peek!

3 **Use a light touch.** Don't go wild coating the basket with nonstick spray, a little spritz is all you need. Too much oil will burn in the heat and start smoking.

4 **Clean up after yourself.** Make sure you scrub the basket with lots of soap and hot water, then dry it completely before using it again. A buildup of oil and food will just begin to burn and cause problems.

HOW TO MAKE IT EXTRA CRISPY

STOCK UP

A stocked pantry is the foundation for every recipe. Here are all the things you'll need for smooth sailing through this book!

BAKING AISLE

Active dry yeast
All-purpose flour
Baking powder
Baking soda
Cocoa powder
Cornstarch
Sugars
  Confectioners'
  Granulated
  Dark brown
Vanilla extract

FRIDGE

Cream cheese
Heavy cream
Large eggs
Milk of choice
Sour cream
Unsalted butter

DRY GOODS

Crushed tomatoes
Dijon mustard
Honey
Maple syrup
Marinara
Mayonnaise
Oils
  Extra-virgin olive oil
  Nonstick spray
  Vegetable oil
Panko breadcrumbs
Ramen
Soy sauce
Spaghetti
Sweetened
  condensed milk
Vegetable stock
Vinegars
  Apple
  Rice
  White

SPICES

Black pepper
Dried herbs
  Chives
  Dill
  Italian seasoning
  Oregano
  Parsley
Ground spices
  Chili powder
  Cinnamon
  Cloves
  Cumin
  Garlic powder
  Onion powder
  Paprika
Kosher salt
Red pepper flakes

THE MELLO WAY

I like my kitchen to be an exciting place loaded with lots of flavor. Besides the usual flour, sugar, salt, and oil, here are my favorite staples I keep in stock at all times.

MELLO'S TOP 10
PANTRY COUNTDOWN

10. Fire Cracker: I always keep a box of graham crackers around. Besides being the base for s'mores, they also make an incredible pie crust, mix-in for oatmeal, and even a delicious rim on a drink.

9. Feeling Bubbly: One of my favorite things is bubble tea, so I always keep a bag of boba in my pantry. These little balls come in lots of colors and flavors and I love to mix and match in my drinks.

8. Dye Hard: Nothing brings the fun like food coloring! A few drops are all it takes to make desserts or drinks stand out from the crowd.

7. Ferment to Be: Kimchi is a Korean staple made from fermented vegetables, like cabbage or radish, for a sour, spicy, and savory bite. It's a powerhouse of flavor and texture.

6. Wrap It Up: Flour tortillas are a power player in my kitchen for breakfast, lunch, dinner, and every snack in between. I always keep a fresh pack nearby!

5. Spice Up Your Life: When I need a little fire, I grab two of my favorite Korean products. Gochugaru is chili powder that's spicy but not overwhelming, and gochujang is a fermented chili paste that's a perfect balance of sweet, spicy, and savory.

4. Sweet Dreams Are Made of Cheese: Cheesy food is the best food. I stay ready with plenty of grated Parmesan, shredded mozzarella, American cheese slices, and even cheese dip.

3. Cereal-sly Delicious: Break out of the bowl! I love using cereal as a crunchy, sweet, and colorful topping for some of my favorite breakfast dishes and desserts.

2. Coming in Hot: I'm always snacking on a bag of Flamin' Hot Cheetos, so it's no shock that I love to cook with them too. Crush them up and use them like spicy breadcrumbs for a spicy kick on any dish.

1. The Sweetest Thing: What would this book be if it wasn't loaded with marshmallows?! I always have bags of mini, jumbo, and (my favorite) Stuffed Puffs ready and waiting to help breakfast, dessert, and even drinks hit the sweet spot.

SNACK ATTACK

NORI POPCORN

Salty, savory seaweed snacks are the perfect topping for freshly popped popcorn. Go big with some sesame seeds and a variety of spicy, sweet, or crunchy mix-ins.

½ cup (120g) **popcorn kernels**

1 (0.35-ounce/10g) package **seaweed snacks,** any flavor

2 teaspoons **toasted sesame seeds**

2 teaspoons **black sesame seeds**

½ teaspoon **kosher salt**

1 Add the popcorn kernels to a brown paper lunch bag. Fold the top of the bag over a few times to secure.

2 Microwave on high for 4 to 5 minutes, until the popping slows to 2-second intervals between pops.

3 Remove the bag from the microwave and carefully unfold the top to release the steam.

4 Crush the seaweed snacks in your hands and sprinkle into the popcorn bag. Add the sesame seeds and salt. Pinch the top closed and shake to mix it all together.

5 Serve directly from the bag or pour into a popcorn bowl.

 **MELLO'S REMIX**

Add 1 tablespoon of togarashi (Japanese spice blend) for a spicy kick, 2 teaspoons of dark brown sugar for a sweet note, or 1 cup (57g) of seaweed-wrapped rice crackers for extra crunch.

KICKIN' CHICKEN AND WAFFLE BITES

The brunch classic gets remixed into mini chicken and waffle sandwiches. They're the perfect small bites for any time of day!

FOR THE WAFFLES
1 cup (120g) store-bought **waffle mix,** plus additional ingredients according to box instructions

FOR THE CHICKEN
Canola oil, for frying
4 to 6 **chicken tenderloins**
2 cups (240g) **all-purpose flour,** divided
1 tablespoon **garlic salt**
1½ teaspoons **cayenne**
1½ teaspoons **paprika**
2 teaspoons **poultry seasoning**
2 pinches **black pepper**
1 large **egg**
¾ cup (180ml) **water**
1 teaspoon **salt**

FOR SERVING
Appetizer skewers
Maple syrup

1 **Make the waffles:** Heat a 9-inch (23cm) square waffle maker to medium.

2 To a large bowl, add the waffle mix and prepare according to box instructions.

3 Add enough batter to fill the waffle iron. Close the lid and cook for about 5 minutes, until the waffle is golden brown and steaming. Repeat with the remaining batter.

4 **Make the chicken:** Fill a deep fryer or large pot with oil and heat to 375°F (190°C). In a large shallow dish, combine 1 cup (120g) flour, the garlic salt, cayenne, paprika, poultry seasoning, and a pinch of black pepper.

5 In another shallow dish, whisk together the egg and water; add the remaining 1 cup (120g) flour, salt, and a pinch of black pepper. Dip each piece of chicken in the egg mixture, then turn to coat with the flour mixture.

6 Fry the chicken, several pieces at a time, until the chicken is golden brown and the juices run clear, 7 to 8 minutes on each side. Drain on paper towels.

7 **To serve:** Cut each waffle square into fourths. Cut each chicken tender into fourths. Skewer one piece of chicken between two mini waffle squares.

8 Enjoy immediately with maple syrup drizzled on top or served on the side.

COPYCAT SNACKWRAP

My fast-food fave is super easy to make at home, but the best part is making a big batch of homemade ranch to keep on hand.

FOR THE RANCH

½ cup (113g) **mayonnaise**
¼ cup (57g) **sour cream**
½ teaspoon **dried parsley**
½ teaspoon **dried chives**
½ teaspoon **dried dill**
¼ teaspoon **kosher salt**
¼ teaspoon **garlic powder**
¼ teaspoon **onion powder**

FOR THE CHICKEN

1 pound (454g)
  chicken tenderloins
Kosher salt
1 large **egg**
2 tablespoons homemade or
  store-bought **ranch dressing**
2 cups (150g)
  panko breadcrumbs
1 teaspoon **cornstarch**
Nonstick cooking spray

FOR THE WRAP

4 large **tortillas or wraps**
1 cup (75g) **shredded lettuce**
1 cup (113g) **fiesta cheese blend**

1 **Make the ranch:** In a small bowl, whisk together the mayonnaise, sour cream, parsley, chives, dill, salt, garlic powder, and onion powder. Cover tightly with plastic wrap and refrigerate until ready to use or for up to 3 days.

2 **Make the chicken:** Preheat the oven to 400°F (200°C). Line a rimmed baking sheet with parchment paper.

3 Pat the chicken tenders dry and season both sides with salt. In a medium shallow bowl, whisk the egg and ranch dressing together. In a separate medium shallow bowl, mix the panko and cornstarch together.

4 Dip a chicken tender into the egg mixture to coat completely. Let the excess drip off, then place in the panko. Coat both sides completely and gently press to adhere the panko. Place the tender on the baking sheet and spray both sides with nonstick spray. Repeat with the remaining chicken tenders.

5 Arrange the tenders evenly across the baking sheet and bake for about 15 minutes, flipping the pieces halfway, until golden brown and cooked through. Transfer to a plate and chop into small pieces if desired.

6 **Prepare the wrap:** Layer the center of each tortilla with ranch, lettuce, cheese, chicken, and additional ranch if desired. Fold in both sides, fold the bottom flap over the top, and roll shut. Serve warm.

Break out the air fryer! *After spraying with nonstick spray, arrange the tenders in the fryer basket (in batches if necessary) and set the fryer to 400°F (200°C) for about 8 minutes, until the tenders are golden brown and cooked through, flipping halfway through.*

PREP: 5 MINUTES   **COOK:** 10 MINUTES   **SERVES:** 6 TO 8

"BE KIND" BRIE BRÛLÉE

A gooey wheel of baked brie is already a perfect snack, so the only thing that could make it better is a crispy charred sugar topping. Just remember to be kind and share with friends!

1 (8-ounce/227g) **wheel of brie**
1 tablespoon **sugar**
Drizzle of **honey**
Crackers, fresh fruit, and other **cheese board ingredients**

1 Preheat the oven to 350°F (180°C).

2 Carefully cut off the top rind of the brie and sprinkle with the sugar.

3 Place the brie on a heatproof dish and bake for 8 to 10 minutes, until soft and gooey.

4 Turn the oven to broil and brûlée the top of the brie for 2 to 3 minutes, until caramelized. Alternatively, remove the brie from the oven and use a handheld torch to brûlée the top.

5 Let cool and harden for a few minutes before drizzling with honey and enjoying with your cheese board ingredients.

SPICED AIR-FRIED CHICKPEAS

These chickpeas get tossed in an Indian masala spice blend and are air fried until perfectly crunchy. They're the perfect snack to eat by the handful.

1 (15.5-ounce/439g) can
   chickpeas, drained and rinsed
1 teaspoon **vegetable oil**
1 teaspoon **chaat masala**
Kosher salt

1 Pat the chickpeas completely dry with paper towels, then transfer to a medium bowl. Add the vegetable oil and toss to coat.

2 Arrange the chickpeas in an even layer in an air fryer basket (you might have to do this in two batches if you have a small fryer). Set the fryer to 400°F (200°C) for 10 to 12 minutes, until the chickpeas are golden brown and crispy.

3 Transfer the chickpeas back to the bowl and toss with the chaat masala and a generous pinch of salt. Serve warm.

No air fryer? *Line a rimmed baking sheet with parchment paper and bake the chickpeas in a 400°F (200°C) oven for 20 to 30 minutes.*

☠ MELLO'S REMIX

Take the chickpeas on a world tour by swapping out the chaat masala for sazón, Chinese five spice, za'atar, berbere, or Old Bay seasoning.

BACON CHEDDAR CROISSANTS

These little bites only need four ingredients and take almost no effort to make. The only hard part is waiting for them to cool down.

2 sheets **puff pastry**

⅔ cup (75g) **shredded cheddar**

12 slices **bacon**

1 large **egg,** whisked

2 tablespoons **butter,** melted

2 teaspoons **sesame seeds**

1 Preheat the oven to 400°F (200°C) and line two large baking sheets with parchment paper.

2 Place one puff pastry sheet on each baking sheet and sprinkle on the cheese.

3 Arrange the strips of bacon across each sheet of puff pastry so they are directly next to each other but not overlapping.

4 Slice the puff pastry between each piece of bacon and then twist. Brush with melted butter and sprinkle with sesame seeds.

5 Place in the oven and bake for 20 to 25 minutes, until the puff pastry is golden brown and the bacon is crispy. Let cool for 10 minutes before serving.

FLAMIN' HOT FRIED MOZZARELLA ONION RINGS

Can't decide between mozzarella sticks and onion rings? Have both! The cheese gets layered between the onion, so every bite has the stringy pull you're craving. Flaming-hot dust on the rings and spicy marinara for dipping just up the fun!

FOR THE SPICY MARINARA
1 tablespoon **extra-virgin olive oil**
½ teaspoon **red pepper flakes** (optional)
½ cup (112g) **marinara sauce**

FOR THE ONION RINGS
1 large **white onion**
20 deli slices **low-moisture mozzarella** (about 1 pound/454g)
2 cups (240g) **all-purpose flour**
6 large **eggs**
2 cups (150g) **panko breadcrumbs**
1 cup (28g) **Flamin' Hot Cheetos**, crushed into a powder
1 tablespoon **Italian seasoning**
1 quart (1L) **vegetable oil**
Kosher salt

1. **Make the spicy marinara:** To a small saucepan over medium heat, add the olive oil and red pepper flakes (if using). Cook until the red pepper flakes start to sizzle, about 3 minutes. Add the marinara and stir to combine. Bring to a simmer, then cover and remove from the heat.

2. **Make the onion rings:** Slice the root and top off the onion, then peel the skin. Cut the onion into ½-inch (1cm) rounds and separate all the rings. Match the rings into pairs that fit inside each other with a little space.

3. Cut each mozzarella slice into four even strips. Stack two or three strips on top of each other to wedge between the pairs of onion rings. Continue stacking and adding strips of mozzarella all the way around the ring.

4. In a medium shallow bowl, spread out the flour. In another bowl, whisk the eggs. In a third bowl, mix the panko, Cheetos, and Italian seasoning. Dip a stuffed onion ring into the flour and flip to cover. Move to the egg mixture and turn to coat. Let the excess drip off, then place in the panko. Coat both sides completely and gently press to adhere the panko. Move to a plate and repeat with the remaining onion rings.

5. Heat the vegetable oil in a Dutch oven to 350°F (180°C). Working in batches, fry the rings until golden brown, flipping halfway, about 2 minutes. (Don't fry for too long or the cheese will start leaking out!) Transfer the rings to paper towels to drain, and sprinkle with salt. Continue frying, adjusting the heat to make sure the oil stays at a steady temperature.

6. If needed, warm the marinara over low heat, then pour into a small bowl for dipping. Arrange the rings on a plate and serve.

35 SNACK ATTACK

WHEN **HUNGER STRIKES, FIGHT BACK** WITH A **SNACK ATTACK!**

STUFFED PIZZA POPPERS

These stuffed pizza poppers have a cheesy center, a buttery garlic topping, and a required bowl of pizza sauce for dunking.

One 16-ounce (453g) can
  jumbo biscuits, separated
  into 8 biscuits
16 slices **pepperoni**
3 ounces (85g)
  mozzarella, cut into 16 cubes
3 tablespoons **butter,** melted
1 tablespoon **grated Parmesan**
¼ teaspoon **garlic powder**
¼ teaspoon **Italian seasoning**
Pizza sauce

1 Preheat the oven to 375°F (190°C).

2 Cut each biscuit in half. Gently flatten each piece on a cutting board. Place one slice of pepperoni on each biscuit, then add a cube of mozzarella. Fold the edges of the dough to the center, pinch gently to close any gaps, and use your hands to roll the dough into a ball.

3 In a small bowl, mix the butter, Parmesan, garlic powder, and Italian seasoning. Dip each biscuit ball into the mixture, then place them in a cast-iron skillet.

4 Bake for 18 minutes or until golden brown.

5 Remove from the oven and let cool in the pan. Serve with pizza sauce.

APFELRADLN
(FRIED APPLE RINGS)

This sweet treat from Austria, basically battered-and-fried apple slices, is the most delicious way to eat your fruit. An apfelradln a day keeps the doctor away!

2 large **apples**
1 cup (120g) **all-purpose flour**
1 tablespoon **sugar**
Kosher salt
2 large **eggs**
½ cup (120ml) **milk of choice**
Cooking spray
Cinnamon sugar

1 Preheat a large nonstick skillet over low heat.

2 Peel the apples, then slice the top and bottom off. Cut into ½-inch (1cm) rings. Use a small cookie cutter or bottle cap to cut the cores out of the apple slices.

3 In a medium bowl, whisk together the flour, sugar, and a big pinch of salt. Add the eggs and milk and whisk into a fairly smooth batter (some lumps are okay).

4 Coat the skillet with nonstick spray. Drop an apple ring into the batter and use a fork to flip it so it's completely coated. Lift the ring out of the batter with the fork and let some of the excess drip off, then lay it in the skillet.

5 Repeat with more rings until the skillet is filled, but not crowded. Fry until the bottoms are golden brown, 3 to 4 minutes, then flip and fry until golden, 3 more minutes. Transfer to a plate and continue dipping and frying the remaining rings.

6 Top the fried rings generously with cinnamon sugar before serving.

Break out the air fryer! *Line an air fryer basket with aluminum foil. Working in batches, arrange the battered rings without touching. Set the air fryer to 400°F (200°C) for 5 minutes. Flip and fry for 2 more minutes, until golden brown all over.*

RICE PAPER TTEOKBOKKI
(SPICY KOREAN RICE CAKE SKEWERS)

This version of tteokbokki (spicy Korean rice cakes) is made from rice paper rolls and simmered in a sweet, spicy, salty sauce until caramelized and chewy. It's impossible to eat just one!

8 pieces **rice paper**
¼ cup (60ml) **cold water**
1½ tablespoons **tomato sauce**
1 tablespoon **gochujang**
1 tablespoon **honey**
1 tablespoon **gochugaru**
1½ teaspoons **soy sauce**
1 teaspoon **dark brown sugar**
1 teaspoon **sesame oil**
¼ teaspoon **minced garlic**

SPECIAL EQUIPMENT
Wooden skewers

1 Working one at a time, submerge each piece of rice paper in the cold water for about 3 seconds on each side. Transfer to a flat surface and roll each piece tightly. Cut each cylinder into three pieces. Add three to six pieces to a skewer.

2 In a medium skillet, make the sauce. Add the tomato sauce, gochujang, honey, gochugaru, soy sauce, brown sugar, sesame oil, and garlic. Bring to a simmer.

3 Add the skewers and cook them for 2 minutes on each side, or until caramelized. Enjoy!

AIR-FRIED PAD THAI EGG ROLLS

Dinner or appetizer? Why choose! These crispy egg rolls get stuffed with a pad thai–inspired filling for the best of both worlds.

1 (3-pound/1.4kg) store-bought **plain rotisserie chicken**

¾ cup (240g) store-bought **pad thai sauce,** plus more for serving

1 **red bell pepper,** thinly sliced

1 large **carrot,** grated

2 **scallions,** finely sliced, plus more for garnish

16 **egg roll wrappers**

Cooking spray

Soy sauce

Lime wedges

1 Remove the meat from the chicken and finely shred. Use 2½ cups (350g) for this recipe and save the rest for Twice-Baked Buffalo Chicken Potatoes (page 119) or another recipe of your choice.

2 Add the shredded chicken to a large bowl with the pad thai sauce, bell pepper, carrot, and scallions, and mix to combine.

3 Working one at a time, use your fingers to gently wet the edges of each egg roll wrapper with water, then add a few tablespoons of the chicken filling to the center.

4 Fold the bottom corner of the wrapper up and over the filling. Fold the left and right corners in toward the center. Push the egg roll away from you and roll toward the top corner. Repeat with the remaining wrappers and filling.

5 Preheat your air fryer to 350°F (180°C) for 3 to 4 minutes. In batches, add the egg rolls to the air fryer basket and spray with cooking spray. Cook for 6 to 8 minutes, flipping halfway through, until browned and crispy.

6 Enjoy with more pad thai sauce, soy sauce, and lime wedges on the side!

No air fryer? *Bake these instead! Preheat the oven to 400°F (200°C) and line a rimmed baking sheet with aluminum foil. Spray the rolled egg rolls all over with cooking spray and arrange on the baking sheet. Bake for 20 to 25 minutes, flipping halfway, until golden and crispy.*

AIR-FRIED BBQ TOFU FRIES

These crispy tofu fries get covered in spices for a seasoned fries vibe. After a trip through the air fryer, they're a perfectly crunchy and very addictive snack.

12 ounces (340g) **extra-firm tofu**

1 tablespoon **olive oil**

2 tablespoons **all-purpose flour**

2 tablespoons **nutritional yeast**

2 teaspoons **garlic powder**

1 teaspoon **Italian seasoning**

1 teaspoon **kosher salt**

½ teaspoon **paprika**

¼ teaspoon **cayenne**

3 tablespoons **BBQ sauce**

1 Preheat the air fryer to 400°F (200°C).

2 Cut the tofu into long strips about ½-inch (1.5cm) wide. Add to a medium bowl and toss with olive oil.

3 In a shallow bowl, combine the flour, nutritional yeast, garlic powder, Italian seasoning, salt, paprika, and cayenne.

4 Gently toss the tofu strips with the seasonings to coat.

5 Place the tofu strips in the air fryer basket in a single layer.

6 Air fry for 18 to 22 minutes, flipping halfway, until crispy.

7 Enjoy with BBQ sauce.

No air fryer? *Bake these instead! Preheat the oven to 400°F (200°C) and line a rimmed baking sheet with aluminum foil. Arrange the seasoned tofu on the baking sheet. Bake for 20 to 25 minutes, flipping halfway, until golden and crispy.*

TOASTER HOT POCKETS

This quick and easy version of the after-school classic uses a few ingredients you probably already have in the fridge. It takes just a few minutes in the toaster!

1 large **flour tortilla**
2 slices **deli mozzarella**
2 slices **salami**
2 **fresh basil leaves**
¼ cup (56g) **marinara sauce**

1 Lay out the tortilla on a flat surface. On the edge of the tortilla, stack one slice of cheese, then the salami, then two basil leaves, then top with the other slice of cheese.

2 Fold in the sides of the tortilla, then fold it in half. It should be open on one side and resemble a t-shirt pocket.

3 Cook in the toaster on medium for 4 to 6 minutes, until the outside is golden brown and the cheese is melted.

4 Enjoy with the marinara sauce.

SOFT PRETZEL BITES
(FEAT. HONEY MUSTARD)

These super easy and super soft pretzel bites are an addictive snack. A sweet and tangy honey mustard for dipping makes them even harder to resist!

FOR THE PRETZELS:

¾ cup (180ml) **warm water**

2 teaspoons **sugar**

1 teaspoon **active dry yeast**

2 cups (240g) **all-purpose flour,**
  plus more for dusting

½ teaspoon **kosher salt**

4 cups (1L) **water**

¼ cup (72g) **baking soda**

Flaky sea salt

FOR THE HONEY MUSTARD:

¼ cup (84g) **honey**

¼ cup (57g) **mayonnaise**

¼ cup (60g) **Dijon mustard**

1 tablespoon **white vinegar**

¼ teaspoon **cayenne**

1 **Make the pretzels:** In a large bowl, whisk the warm water and sugar together until the sugar dissolves. Sprinkle the yeast over top and let sit for about 5 minutes, until foamy.

2 Add the flour and salt. Stir with a wooden spoon until a sticky dough forms, then turn onto a lightly floured surface and knead by hand until the dough comes together in a smooth ball, about 5 minutes (or see Take a break!).

3 Return the dough to the bowl and cover tightly with plastic. Set somewhere warm to rise until doubled in size, about 1 hour.

4 Preheat the oven to 400°F (200°C). Line a rimmed baking sheet with parchment paper.

5 Punch the dough down and turn onto a lightly floured surface. Divide the dough into three equal pieces, then roll each piece into a 12-inch-long (30cm) rope. Cut each rope into twelve equal pieces, about 1 inch (2.5cm) wide.

6 To a large pot, add the water and baking soda and bring to a boil over high heat. Working in batches, add the pieces of dough and boil for about 20 seconds, until swollen and floating. Use a slotted spoon to transfer the dough to the baking sheet. Sprinkle with flaky salt while the pretzels are still wet, then continue boiling the rest of the dough in batches.

7 Arrange the pretzels evenly over the baking sheet, then bake for 15 to 20 minutes, until golden brown. Transfer to a plate.

8 **Make the honey mustard:** Whisk the honey, mayonnaise, mustard, vinegar, and cayenne in a small bowl. Serve with the pretzel bites.

Take a break! *The dough can be made in a stand mixer fitted with a dough hook attachment. Knead on medium-high for about 10 minutes, until a smooth dough forms.*

☺ MELLO'S REMIX

Some days you're salty, some days you're sweet.
To make sweet pretzels, whisk 1 cup (220g) sugar and 3 tablespoons
ground cinnamon in a large bowl. Bake the pretzel bites without the
flaky salt and brush them with 6 tablespoons (85g) melted butter as
soon as they come out of the oven. Toss the pretzels in the bowl with
the cinnamon sugar and serve with frosting for dipping.

AIR-FRIED SPINACH ARTICHOKE BREAD BOWL DIP

Everyone's favorite appetizer gets the air fryer treatment in this super easy recipe. While the bread gets toasty, the filling gets super gooey and ready for dipping!

1 (14-ounce/397g) can **artichoke hearts,** drained and chopped

8 ounces (227g) **frozen spinach,** thawed, drained, and chopped (about 1¼ cups)

4 ounces (113g) **cream cheese,** at room temperature

2 cups (226g) **shredded mozzarella**

½ cup (120g) **sour cream**

¼ cup (57g) **mayonnaise**

¼ cup (25g) **grated Parmesan**

2 **garlic cloves,** minced

1 round loaf **bread**

1 Preheat the air fryer to 375°F (190°C).

2 Mix the artichoke hearts, spinach, cream cheese, mozzarella, sour cream, mayonnaise, Parmesan, and garlic in a large bowl.

3 Use a bread knife to slice off the top of the bread. Scoop out the bread and cut or tear the insides into small pieces.

4 Pour the dip into the bread bowl and air-fry for 12 to 15 minutes, until the cheese has melted and the top is golden brown.

5 Serve, using the small pieces of bread to dip into the spinach and artichoke dip.

No air fryer? *Bake this instead! Preheat the oven to 375°F (190°C) and line a rimmed baking sheet with aluminum foil. Pour the dip into the bread bowl and place on the baking sheet. Bake for 15 to 20 minutes, until the cheese has melted and the bread is golden brown.*

BREAKFAST CLUB

CRAZY-FLUFFY JAPANESE PANCAKES

Japanese pancakes are like fluffy little clouds. The whipped egg whites make these more like a soufflé in pancake form, meaning breakfast just got extra delicious!

4 large **eggs**
¾ cup (90g) **all-purpose flour**
½ cup (120ml) **whole milk**
¼ cup (50g) **sugar**
1 teaspoon **baking powder**
Nonstick cooking spray
Unsalted butter
Maple syrup
Fresh blueberries, optional

SPECIAL EQUIPMENT
3-inch (7.5cm) **ring molds** or **biscuit cutters**

1 Preheat the oven to 250°F (120°C). Preheat a large nonstick skillet over low heat.

2 Set two medium bowls on the counter. Crack the eggs and divide four egg whites in one bowl and two egg yolks in the other bowl. (Discard the other two yolks or reserve for another use.) Use a whisk or a handheld mixer to beat the egg whites to stiff peaks.

3 Add the flour, milk, sugar, and baking powder to the bowl with yolks and whisk to combine. Use a rubber spatula to transfer about a quarter of the egg whites to the batter and fold to combine so the batter feels light and fluffy. Add the remaining egg whites and gently fold to just incorporate, making sure the batter stays big and fluffy in the bowl.

4 Spray the skillet and ring molds thoroughly with nonstick spray. Set the ring molds in the skillet, then scoop ½ cup (120ml) of batter into each mold. Cover and cook on low heat until the pancakes are almost completely set, about 10 minutes. Use a spatula to flip the molds and cook, uncovered, until set, about 2 minutes. Transfer to an oven-safe plate and keep warm in the oven while making the rest of the pancakes.

5 Divide the pancakes among plates and serve with plenty of butter, maple syrup, and fresh blueberries, if using.

EXTRA "FLY" FLUFFERNUTTER FRENCH TOAST

There's French toast, and then there's the extra-fly flavors of French toast stuffed with peanut butter and marshmallows, coated in crushed cereal, and cooked until crispy on the outside and super gooey on the inside. Which team are you on?

3 cups (180g) **Cinnamon Toast Crunch cereal**

8 slices **sandwich bread**

½ cup (135g) **creamy peanut butter**

8 **stuffed marshmallows,** such as Stuffed Puffs, any flavor

1 large **egg**

½ cup (120ml) **half and half**

2 tablespoons **sugar**

Kosher salt

Cooking spray

Unsalted butter

Warm **maple syrup**

 **MELLO'S REMIX**

If you're not a fan of peanut butter, remix this track with jam, Nutella, apple butter, pumpkin puree, or cookie butter. Marshmallows are optional, but still highly recommended!

1 Preheat the oven to 250°F (120°C). Set a rimmed baking sheet in the oven to preheat.

2 Add the cereal to a large ziplock bag, and using a rolling pin, crush the cereal into a fine meal. Transfer to a plate and set aside. Reserve ½ cup (120g) for serving.

3 Lay out the slices of bread and spread the peanut butter evenly on one side of each slice. Place two marshmallows on four of the slices of bread, then sandwich them with the other four slices. Press gently to adhere.

4 In a medium shallow bowl, whisk together the egg, half and half, sugar, and a big pinch of salt.

5 Place a large nonstick skillet over low heat and coat with cooking spray. Place one of the sandwiches in the batter for about 5 seconds, then flip to coat the other side for 5 seconds. Use a spatula to lift the sandwich from the batter, letting the excess drip away, and place in the crushed cereal. Coat both sides and then transfer to the skillet. Repeat with a second sandwich.

6 Fry until the bottoms of the sandwiches are golden brown, about 4 minutes, then flip and fry until the marshmallows start to melt, about 4 more minutes. Transfer to the baking sheet in the oven and repeat with the remaining two sandwiches.

7 Divide the French toast among plates and top with butter, maple syrup, and more crushed cereal before serving.

WAFFLE MAKER HASHBROWNS

The best part about classic diner hashbrowns is the extra crispy edges. And what's the easiest way to go big on crispy? Throw them in a waffle maker!

4 slices **bacon**, halved

4 **eggs**

1 (16-ounce/453g) bag (4 cups) **frozen hashbrowns,** thawed

1 cup (110g) **shredded cheddar**

¼ cup (11g) chopped **chives**, plus more for serving

1 teaspoon **garlic powder**

1 teaspoon **paprika**

Kosher salt

Black pepper

Cooking spray

Fried eggs, optional

1 Preheat your waffle maker to medium, then add the bacon. Cook for 5 to 7 minutes, until the bacon is cooked to desired crispiness. Place on a paper towel to drain, then chop into small pieces. Drain the excess bacon fat out of the waffle maker.

2 In a large bowl, whisk the eggs. Add the hashbrowns, cheddar, bacon, chives, garlic powder, paprika, salt, and pepper. Mix to combine.

3 Heat the waffle maker to medium heat. Add 1 cup (125g) of the batter and spread into an even layer. Cook for 5 to 7 minutes, until crispy. Repeat for the remaining batter.

4 Sprinkle with more chives and enjoy alone or topped with fried eggs, if desired.

POTATO CHIP OMELET
(ANY FLAVOR REMIX)

Wild on paper, but delicious on the plate! The chips get a little soft as they cook, almost like thinly sliced potatoes. I love to mix and match all my favorite flavors.

6 large **eggs**

½ cup (120ml) **half and half** or **whole milk**

Kosher salt

Black pepper

4 cups (136g) **potato chips,** any flavor

1 tablespoon **unsalted butter**

1 tablespoon roughly chopped **fresh parsley**

1 In a large bowl, add the eggs, half and half, and a large pinch of salt and pepper. Whisk until the eggs are completely smooth, about 2 minutes. Add the chips to the bowl and use a spatula to fold them in (a little crushing is fine, but try to keep them intact).

2 Melt the butter in a medium nonstick skillet over medium heat. Add the egg mixture, using the spatula to spread out the chips evenly across the skillet. Cover immediately and cook until the omelet is just slightly runny on top, about 5 minutes. Remove from the heat and let sit, still covered, until the eggs are fully set, about 3 more minutes.

3 Top with the parsley, then slide the omelet onto a cutting board or large plate before slicing and serving.

🐾 MELLO'S REMIX

My favorite chips for this omelet are barbecue, sour cream and onion, salt and vinegar, or flamin' hot for a spicy kick, but use whatever you like!

"SILENCE" S'MORES OVERNIGHT OATS

There's nothing better than waking up to a gift that yesterday you made for today you. Having these overnight oats waiting in the fridge will make the morning so much sweeter!

1 cup (90g) **old-fashioned rolled oats**

1 cup (240ml) **milk of choice**

½ cup (114g) **Greek yogurt**

3 tablespoons **cocoa powder**

3 tablespoons **honey, maple syrup,** or **agave**

2 tablespoons **chia seeds**

¼ cup (32g) **marshmallow fluff,** plus more for topping

Chocolate syrup, for drizzling

¼ cup (36g) crushed **graham crackers,** plus more for topping

2 **stuffed marshmallows,** such as Stuffed Puffs, any flavor

1 Set out two pint jars or airtight containers and evenly divide the oats, milk, yogurt, cocoa powder, honey, and chia seeds into each jar. Stir to combine.

2 Add the marshmallow fluff, chocolate syrup, and graham crackers to each jar and gently stir.

3 Close each jar or container tightly and refrigerate overnight or for up to 5 days.

4 Before serving, cut the marshmallows into small pieces.

5 Remove from the refrigerator and top with the marshmallows, more fluff, more chocolate, and more graham crackers before serving.

☠ MELLO'S REMIX

Instead of yogurt, use your favorite flavor of ice cream at the bottom of the jar. The ice cream will melt overnight in the fridge, making an extra creamy and delicious treat in the morning.

PREP: 10 MINUTES **COOK:** 10 MINUTES **SERVES:** 2

LOADED CHILAQUILES
(FEAT. CRISPY GARLIC EGGS)

Chilaquiles—basically tortilla chips drowning in salsa—are one of the greatest breakfast inventions of all time. Just like nachos, there's no wrong answer for what you can pile on top. I like mine with crispy fried eggs and all the classic fixings.

FOR THE CHILAQUILES

4 cups (104g) **flavored tortilla chips,** such as Doritos

2 cups (480ml) **enchilada sauce** (red or green or 1 cup/240ml of each)

1 tablespoon **vegetable oil**

Kosher salt

Black pepper

FOR THE CRISPY GARLIC EGGS

1 tablespoon **olive oil**

6 **garlic cloves,** thinly sliced

2 large **eggs**

FOR TOPPING

Crumbled **cotija**

Thinly sliced **scallions**

Fresh cilantro leaves

Thinly sliced **radishes**

Sliced **avocado**

Crema

Lime wedges

1 Preheat the oven to 400°F (200°C).

2 **Make the chilaquiles:** Arrange the chips on a medium oven-safe skillet. Spoon the enchilada sauce over the chips (if using both red and green enchilada sauce, do one side red and one side green). Bake for about 10 minutes, until the chips and salsa are warm.

3 **Make the crispy garlic eggs:** Heat the oil in a medium nonstick skillet over medium-high heat until it shimmers. Add in the garlic and cook until lightly golden, 1 to 2 minutes. Push the garlic to one side of the skillet and crack in the eggs. Immediately add the garlic to the tops of the eggs and cook until the whites are set, about 3 minutes.

4 Cover the chilaquiles with your toppings, finish with the eggs, and serve immediately.

MELLO'S REMIX

Remix your breakfast with a tostilocos-inspired spin. After baking the chips and sauce, top with diced cucumber and jicama, hot sauce, chamoy, Tajín, Japanese peanuts, and plenty of lime wedges. Fried eggs are optional, but still totally delicious.

BACON AND EGG JIANBING

Jianbing is a Chinese street food classic. It's a breakfast crêpe made with a thin layer of batter and stuffed with egg, chili sauce, and veggies. Think of it as the original fast food!

¼ cup (30g) **all-purpose flour**

2 tablespoons **whole wheat flour**

¼ teaspoon **Chinese five spice**

¼ teaspoon **kosher salt**

½ cup (120ml) **water,** plus more as needed

Cooking spray

2 large **eggs**

1 **scallion,** thinly sliced

1 teaspoon **black or white sesame seeds**

1 tablespoon **chili crisp**

2 slices cooked **bacon,** cut into 1-inch (2.5cm) pieces

¼ cup (32g) **bean sprouts** or **microgreens**

1 Preheat a large nonstick skillet over low heat.

2 In a medium bowl, whisk together the all-purpose flour, whole wheat flour, five spice powder, and salt. Add the water and whisk into a smooth, runny batter. Add more water as needed, 1 tablespoon at a time, to reach a runny consistency.

3 Coat the skillet with cooking spray. Pour in the batter and let it set for about 10 seconds, then tilt the skillet to spread it to the edges. Crack the eggs on top of the batter, then use a spatula to break the yolks and spread the eggs to the edges. Sprinkle the scallion and sesame seeds over the eggs. Cover and cook until the bottom and edges of the top are set, about 5 minutes.

4 Slide a spatula under the jianbing and flip. Spread the chili crisp all over the top, then sprinkle the bacon pieces and bean sprouts down the center. Cook until the bottom is set, about 2 minutes more, then use the spatula to fold the two edges without bacon over the center.

5 Slide the jianbing onto a cutting board and slice across the middle to create two long pieces. Stack the pieces on top of each other and wrap in parchment, folding the bottom up to secure in a parchment pouch. Enjoy on the go!

"CHASING STARS" CEREAL MILK CINNAMON ROLLS

The best part about breakfast is there are no rules. Sometimes your cereal looks like mini pancakes; sometimes your cinnamon rolls have cereal on top. As long as it's delicious, who cares!

FOR THE ROLLS
Cooking spray
All-purpose flour, for dusting
2 pounds (907g) **store-bought pizza dough** or **dough from "Shockwave" Stuffed Supreme Pizza (page 90),** room temperature
8 tablespoons (113g) **unsalted butter,** melted, divided
2 cups (426g) packed **light brown sugar**
3 tablespoons **ground cinnamon**
¼ teaspoon **ground cloves**
1 large **egg,** beaten
1 cup (60g) **Fruity Pebbles**

FOR THE ICING
3 cups (340g) **confectioners' sugar**
3 to 5 tablespoons **milk**
1 teaspoon **pure vanilla extract**

1 **Make the rolls:** Preheat the oven to 350°F (180°C). Coat a 9 x 13-inch (23 x 33cm) baking dish with cooking spray.

2 Sprinkle some flour on a work surface, then roll the pizza dough into a 9 x 13-inch (23 x 33cm) rectangle with the shorter side closest to you. Add more flour as needed while rolling. Brush about half of the melted butter over the dough.

3 In a medium bowl, whisk the brown sugar, cinnamon, and cloves until combined. Sprinkle the mixture over the dough, then drizzle the remaining butter on top.

4 Use the short edge in front of you to roll the dough into a tight log. Slice the log into nine 1-inch (2.5cm) rolls. Arrange the rolls in the baking dish, leaving a little space between each one. Cover the dish with plastic wrap and let the dough rise for about 30 minutes, until the rolls are puffy.

5 Discard the plastic wrap and brush the tops of the rolls with the beaten egg. Bake for 30 to 40 minutes, until the rolls are golden brown and the filling is gooey. Sprinkle the Fruity Pebbles on top and cool in the baking dish for 30 minutes.

6 **Make the icing:** In a medium bowl, whisk the confectioners' sugar, 3 tablespoons milk, and the vanilla. Continue adding milk, 1 tablespoon at a time, until the icing is thick but a little runny. Spoon the icing over the rolls and let it melt. Serve warm.

COME ON, JOIN THE BREAKFAST CLUB!

EGG MELLOMUFFIN

When it comes to breakfast sandwiches, there's one that rules them all. But why waste time in the drive-thru when you can make one at home? This is breakfast done the Mello way!

1 tablespoon **unsalted butter**
1 **English muffin**
1 slice **American cheese**
Cooking spray
1 slice **Canadian bacon**
1 large **egg**
Kosher salt

SPECIAL EQUIPMENT
3-inch (7.5cm) **ring mold** or **biscuit cutter**

1 Melt the butter in a medium skillet over medium heat. Split the English muffin in half and lay the cut sides down in the skillet, swirling to coat them in butter. Toast until lightly golden brown, 2 to 3 minutes. Transfer to a plate and lay the cheese on one half.

2 Spray the inside of the ring mold with cooking spray. With the skillet still over medium heat, lay the Canadian bacon on one side and set the ring mold on the other side. Crack the egg into the ring mold. Let the bacon and egg fry until the egg white starts to set, about 2 minutes. Flip the bacon, then remove the skillet from the heat and cover. Let sit until the egg white is set but the yolk is still runny and the bacon is warm and golden brown, about 3 minutes.

3 Remove the ring mold and lay the fried egg over the cheese on the English muffin. Season with salt. Lay the bacon on top of the egg, then add the top half of the English muffin. Serve immediately.

Break out the air fryer! *Line an air fryer basket with aluminum foil. Arrange the Canadian bacon, English muffin halves, and ring mold in the basket. Coat everything with cooking spray. Crack the egg into the ring mold. Set the air fryer to 350°F (180°C) for 5 minutes, until the egg white is set and the English muffin and bacon are golden brown.*

Hot tip! *If you don't like your yolk runny, do this instead: Crack the egg into the ring mold. Let the bacon and egg fry until the white of the egg is starting to set, about 2 minutes. Flip the bacon, then remove the ring mold from the egg and flip it. Remove the skillet from the heat and cover it. Let it sit until the egg is set and the bacon is warm and golden brown, about 3 minutes.*

ACAÍ PROTEIN BOWL

I'm all for fun and games, but sometimes you need a healthy breakfast to fuel your day. This bowl is packed with everything good to get you going and everything delicious to keep you diving in!

2 (7-ounce/200 g) packets **frozen acaí puree**

1 cup (140g) **frozen blueberries**

1 handful **frozen spinach**

½ cup (120ml) **almond milk**

½ cup (114g) **Greek yogurt,** any flavor

1 scoop **protein powder,** any flavor

FOR TOPPING

Granola

2 tablespoons **hemp seed hearts**

2 tablespoons **coconut flakes**

Fresh **fruit**, such as sliced **bananas**

1 To a blender, add the acaí, blueberries, spinach, almond milk, yogurt, and protein powder. Blend until smooth.

2 Top with your favorite toppings.

"SAH SAH" SHAKSHUKA

Shakshuka is a wildly popular (and wildly easy) dish of spiced tomato sauce with poached eggs. It's a perfect breakfast to feed a group!

2 tablespoons **olive oil**

1 medium **white onion,** finely chopped

4 **garlic cloves,** minced

1 tablespoon **smoked paprika**

1 teaspoon **ground cumin**

¼ teaspoon **red pepper flakes** (optional)

1 (28-ounce/794g) can **crushed tomatoes**

Kosher salt

Black pepper

6 large **eggs**

4 ounces (113g) **goat cheese**

2 tablespoons finely chopped **fresh cilantro**

2 tablespoons finely chopped **fresh dill**

2 tablespoons finely chopped **fresh mint**

1 Heat the oil in a large skillet over medium heat until it shimmers. Add the onion and cook, stirring occasionally, until slightly softened, about 5 minutes. Add the garlic, paprika, cumin, and red pepper flakes, if using, and cook until fragrant, about 1 more minute. Add the tomatoes and simmer until the sauce is thick and bubbling, 10 to 12 minutes. Season with salt and black pepper.

2 Use a wooden spoon to make six small wells in the sauce. Crack an egg into a small bowl and then gently pour the egg into a well. Repeat with the remaining eggs. Cover the skillet and cook until the whites are just set and the yolks still look soft, 8 to 10 minutes.

3 Remove the skillet from the heat. Crumble the goat cheese and sprinkle the cilantro, dill, and mint over the top. Serve the shakshuka directly from the skillet.

Hot tip! *Cracking the eggs into a bowl before adding to the pan will help avoid shells in your food.*

MAPLE BACON DONUTS

Maple and bacon are one of the most iconic duos of all time: They just belong together. These little donuts get covered in a maple glaze and topped with crispy bacon for a sweet-salty explosion in every bite.

FOR THE DONUTS
Cooking spray
2 cups (240g) **all-purpose flour**
1½ cups (297g) **granulated sugar**
2 teaspoons **baking powder**
1 teaspoon **apple pie spice** or **pumpkin pie spice**
½ teaspoon **kosher salt**
1 cup (240ml) **whole milk**
1 large **egg,** beaten
2 tablespoons **unsalted butter,** melted

FOR THE ICING
½ cup (120ml) **maple syrup**
2 tablespoons **unsalted butter,** melted
2 cups (227g) **confectioners' sugar**
8 slices cooked **bacon,** cooled and broken into 2-inch (5cm) pieces

SPECIAL EQUIPMENT
2 **donut pans**

1 **Make the donuts:** Preheat the oven to 350°F (180°C). Thoroughly coat two donut pans with cooking spray.

2 In a large bowl, whisk the flour, sugar, baking powder, apple pie spice, and salt. Add the milk, egg, and butter, and use a rubber spatula to fold into a loose batter. Spoon about 2 tablespoons of batter into each donut cup.

3 Bake for 15 to 20 minutes, until the donuts are golden brown and puffy and a toothpick comes out clean. Cool in the pan for 10 minutes before flipping the pan over to release the donuts. Arrange on a wire rack to cool completely, about 30 minutes.

4 **Make the icing:** In a medium bowl, whisk the maple syrup and butter. Add the confectioners' sugar and whisk to form a smooth and slightly stiff icing that runs slowly off the whisk.

5 Dip each donut in the icing and place on the rack. Immediately place two pieces of bacon on top of each donut before the icing sets. Repeat with the remaining donuts and bacon.

MELLO'S REMIX

Instead of maple icing, try another flavor:

Chocolate	Berry	PB
¼ cup (21g) cocoa powder	¼ cup (85g) jam, any flavor	¼ cup (68g) peanut butter
2 cups (227g) confectioners' sugar	2 cups (227g) confectioners' sugar	2 cups (227g) confectioners' sugar
2 to 3 tablespoons milk	1 to 2 tablespoons milk	1 to 2 tablespoons milk

And swap out the bacon for toasted coconut flakes, diced candied ginger, freeze-dried fruit, or chopped nuts!

MATZO BREI BREAKFAST BURRITO

Matzo brei is a genius invention: crumbled matzo mixed into scrambled eggs. But you know I love to go big, so why not turn it into a whole breakfast burrito? The matzo adds the perfect crunch!

FOR THE MATZO BREI
1 piece **matzo**
2 large **eggs**
1 teaspoon **dried chives**
Kosher salt
Black pepper
2 tablespoons **unsalted butter**

FOR THE BURRITO
1 large **flour tortilla**
⅓ cup (28g) **shredded Monterey Jack**
¼ cup (64g) **salsa**
Sliced avocado and cooked **vegan sausage** (optional)

1 Preheat the oven to 350°F (180°C).

2 **Make the matzo brei:** Run the matzo under cold water to wet it. Set it on a plate to soften. In a small bowl, whisk the eggs with the chives and a big pinch of salt and black pepper. Crumble the matzo into the egg mixture.

3 Melt the butter in a small skillet over medium heat. Pour in the egg mixture and use a rubber spatula to swirl to create big curds. Cook until the scrambled eggs are just set, about 2 minutes, then transfer to a plate.

4 **Make the burrito:** Lay the tortilla on a rimmed baking sheet. Spread the cheese evenly over the top, then spread the salsa over the cheese. Bake for about 2 minutes, until the tortilla is soft and the cheese is starting to melt. Arrange the avocado and sausage (if using) along the center, then pile the matzo brei on top.

5 Fold the sides over the filling, then roll from the bottom up to make a tight burrito. Slice in half and serve immediately.

☠ MELLO'S REMIX

Swap out the matzo for crushed tortilla chips, potato chips, or other snacks like Fritos, Cheetos, or Cheez-Its. No need to soak them, they're ready to go and delicious in any flavor!

FLAPJACKS WITH "FRIENDS"

Why have one or two pancakes when you can have a whole bowl of them?! These mini pancakes are adorable, delicious, and perfect to share with friends!

FOR THE SYRUP
½ cup (120ml) **maple syrup**
½ cup (70g) fresh or frozen **blueberries**

FOR THE PANCAKES
2 cups (240g) **all-purpose flour**
3 tablespoons **sugar**
2 teaspoons **baking powder**
1 teaspoon **baking soda**
1 teaspoon **kosher salt**
2½ cups (600ml) **buttermilk**
4 tablespoons **unsalted butter,** melted
2 large **eggs**
Cooking spray
Whipped cream

1 **Make the syrup:** Add the maple syrup and blueberries to a small saucepan over low heat. When the syrup starts to simmer, after about 4 minutes, remove from the heat and cover. The blueberries will soften and burst as they sit.

2 **Make the pancakes:** Preheat the oven to 250°F (120°C). Set a rimmed baking sheet in the oven to preheat.

3 In a large bowl, whisk together the flour, sugar, baking powder, baking soda, and salt. Add the buttermilk, butter, and eggs and whisk until just combined. (Some lumps are okay!)

4 Transfer the batter into a squeeze bottle and set aside. You can also use a small spoon to ladle the batter into the skillet.

5 Set a medium nonstick skillet over low heat for 2 to 3 minutes. Coat with cooking spray, then create small pancakes around the skillet by squeezing out small portions of batter (about ½ tablespoon of batter per pancake). Let cook until bubbles form on the surface and the bottom is golden brown, 1 to 2 minutes. Flip and cook until the pancakes are cooked through, 1 to 2 minutes. Transfer to the baking sheet in the oven and repeat with the rest of the batter, greasing the skillet after each batch.

6 Set the syrup over low heat to rewarm, if needed.

7 Divide the pancakes among bowls and spoon over the syrup and whipped cream.

☺☺ MELLO'S REMIX

You've heard of breakfast for dinner, but what about dessert for breakfast? Stack your pancakes and then go full sundae with a scoop of your favorite ice cream, drizzles of chocolate and caramel sauce, and melted marshmallows! Whipped cream and sprinkles are required for a truly balanced breakfast.

"BYE BYE" BREAKFAST CUPS

Enjoy these on the go for a quick, filling breakfast. They're perfect for those mornings when you're running out the door!

Cooking spray

1 (16-ounce/453g) bag **frozen hashbrowns,** thawed

¾ cup (80g) **shredded cheddar**

4 tablespoons **butter,** melted

Kosher salt

Black pepper

12 large **eggs**

1 cup (130g) chopped precooked **chicken breakfast sausage**

Sliced **scallions**

1 Preheat the oven to 400°F (200°C) and spray a 12-cup muffin pan with cooking spray.

2 To a large bowl, add the hashbrowns, cheddar, and butter. Season with salt and pepper and mix to combine.

3 Evenly divide the mixture into the muffin cups. Press the mixture down and up the sides to create a hole to eventually crack in the eggs.

4 Bake for 20 to 25 minutes, then remove from the oven. Use a spoon or small measuring cup to press down the center of the cups again if needed, then crack an egg into the center of each cup. Add the chicken sausage and season with salt and pepper.

5 Bake for 12 to 15 minutes more, until the eggs are fully cooked.

6 Let cool for 15 minutes. Use a butter knife to carefully remove them from the muffin pan.

7 Sprinkle scallions on top and enjoy! Store leftovers in the fridge for up to 5 days and enjoy as the perfect breakfast on the go.

DIG IN

"SHOCKWAVE" STUFFED SUPREME PIZZA

A loaded supreme pizza is always the right move, but this one has a cheesy surprise hidden in the crust!

FOR THE DOUGH

1 (¼-ounce/7g) packet **active dry yeast**

1 tablespoon **sugar**

2 cups (480ml) **warm water**

2 tablespoons **extra-virgin olive oil**, plus more for drizzling

2 teaspoons **kosher salt**

4 cups (480g) **all-purpose flour**

FOR THE PIZZA

10 sticks **mozzarella string cheese**

3 cups (339g) shredded **mozzarella**

1 (24-ounce/710ml) jar **marinara or pizza sauce**

20 slices **pepperoni**

Extra-virgin olive oil

½ cup (50g) grated **Parmesan**

1 teaspoon **dried oregano**

Fresh basil and oregano

1 **Make the dough:** To a large bowl, add the yeast, sugar, and warm water. Let sit for 5 minutes, until the surface is foamy. Add the oil and salt and use a wooden spoon to briefly stir. Add the flour and stir until a sticky dough comes together. Drizzle a little oil on the dough and use your hands to shape it into a ball.

2 Cover the bowl with plastic wrap and refrigerate for at least 8 hours or up to 24 hours. The dough will slowly rise.

3 Remove the dough from the refrigerator and punch it down. Let it rest at room temperature, uncovered, for about 20 minutes, until soft and pliable. Oil a baking sheet, then spread the dough over the baking sheet, gently stretching it to the edges. (It's okay if it doesn't stretch all the way.) Cover with a kitchen towel and let it rise for 30 minutes, until puffy.

4 **Make the pizza:** Stretch the dough out again, over the edges of the baking sheet. Place the string cheese around the edges of the pan, then fold the dough over the cheese and press down to create a stuffed crust.

5 Preheat the oven to 500°F (260°C).

6 Top the dough with half of the mozzarella and then spoon the marinara over the cheese, then top with the remaining mozzarella. Cut half of the pepperoni pieces into the shape of Marshmello's face. Place the pepperoni over the mozzarella. Drizzle the crust with oil, then sprinkle the Parmesan and oregano on top.

7 Bake for 20 to 25 minutes, until the crust is golden brown and the cheese is just starting to brown. Top with fresh basil and oregano, cut into slices, and serve straight from the pan.

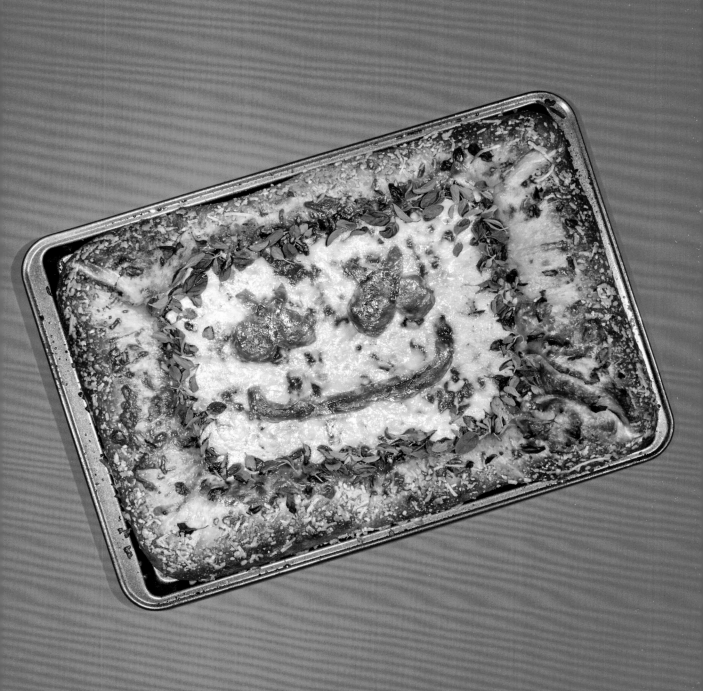

SPICY BAJA SHRIMP TACO BOWLS

The worst part of a shrimp taco is that it's over too soon. These crispy taco bowls keep the party going for a jumbo shrimp experience with all the Baja-inspired flavors I love!

FOR THE TORTILLA BOWLS
4 large **flour tortillas**
Cooking spray

FOR THE COOLING CREMA
½ cup (114g) **sour cream**
¼ cup (60ml) **lime juice**
¼ cup (57g) **mayonnaise**
½ teaspoon **kosher salt**

FOR THE SHRIMP AND SLAW
1 cup (120g) **all-purpose flour**
¼ cup (28g) **cornstarch**
1 tablespoon **baking powder**
2 tablespoons **adobo seasoning**
  or **chili powder,** divided
2 tablespoons **hot sauce,** divided
2½ cups (600ml) **water**
1 pound (454g) **jumbo shrimp,**
  peeled and deveined
2 cups (180g) thinly sliced **red and
  green cabbage**
2 tablespoons **apple cider vinegar**
Kosher salt
1 quart (1L) **vegetable oil**

FOR SERVING
Sliced **avocado**
Fresh cilantro leaves
Shredded **Mexican cheese**
Pickled jalapeños
Chopped **tomato**

1 Preheat your air fryer to 350°F (180°C).

2 **Make the tortilla bowls:** Spray both sides of the tortilla with cooking spray and place into a medium oven-safe bowl. Use your hands to press the tortilla into a bowl shape. Place a slightly smaller oven-safe bowl on top of the tortilla.

3 Place in the air fryer for 5 minutes, then carefully remove the outer bowl and air-fry for another 3 to 4 minutes, until crispy. Set aside to firm up. Repeat with the remaining tortillas.

4 **Make the crema:** Mix the sour cream, lime juice, mayonnaise, and salt in a small bowl.

5 **Make the shrimp:** In a large bowl, whisk the flour, cornstarch, baking powder, and 1 tablespoon each of the adobo seasoning and hot sauce. Add the water and whisk to form a smooth batter.

6 In a small bowl, toss the shrimp with the remaining 1 tablespoon each of the adobo seasoning and hot sauce.

7 **Make the slaw:** In a medium bowl, toss the cabbage, vinegar, and a big pinch of salt. Set aside to marinate.

8 Heat the vegetable oil in a Dutch oven to 350°F (180°C). Working in batches, use tongs to toss a few shrimp in the batter, coating completely. Let the excess batter drip off, then transfer the shrimp to the hot oil. Fry until golden brown, about 4 minutes, flipping halfway. Transfer to paper towels to drain, and sprinkle with a pinch of salt. Continue frying in batches, adjusting the heat to make sure the oil stays at a steady temperature.

9 To the tortilla bowls, add the slaw and top with the fried shrimp, toppings, and crema.

WATERMELON POKE BOWL
(VEGAN REMIX)

This easy poke bowl comes with one big twist: Instead of raw fish, watermelon is the main attraction! After marinating, the watermelon is soft and flavorful; it's a perfect match for all the sweet and spicy flavors in this bowl.

2 tablespoons **mirin**

2 tablespoons **toasted sesame oil**

2 tablespoons **soy sauce or tamari**

2 tablespoons unseasoned **rice vinegar**

Juice of 1 **lime**

4 cups (1L) cubed **watermelon**, in ½-inch (1cm) pieces, from a 3-pound (1.3kg) watermelon

½ cup (113g) vegan **mayonnaise**

2 tablespoons **sriracha**

FOR SERVING

Cooked **white rice**

Matchstick **carrots**

Sliced mini **cucumbers**

Sliced **avocado**

Shelled **edamame**

Thinly sliced **scallions**

Toasted **sesame seeds**

1 In a large bowl, whisk the mirin, sesame oil, soy sauce, vinegar, and lime juice together. Add the watermelon and toss to coat. Cover with plastic wrap and marinate for 30 minutes at room temperature or in the refrigerator for up to 1 hour.

2 In a small bowl, whisk the mayonnaise and sriracha together. Transfer to a small ziplock bag or squeeze bottle and refrigerate until ready to use.

3 Spread the rice along the bottom of four bowls. Use a slotted spoon to scoop and divide the watermelon over the rice. Add carrots, cucumbers, avocado, edamame, scallions, and sesame seeds. Snip the edge off the ziplock bag and squeeze the spicy mayo over each bowl before serving.

JUMBO SPAGHETTI MEATBALL

This spaghetti-stuffed meatball is spaghetti and meatballs in its ultimate form. Pretty much the most impressive and delicious thing you could serve a crowd!

1 pound (454g) **spaghetti**

1 (24-ounce/680g) jar **marinara sauce,** divided

4 pounds (1.8kg) **ground beef**

1½ cups (168g) **Italian breadcrumbs**

3 large **eggs**

¾ cup (180ml) **whole milk**

1 cup (100g) **grated Parmesan,** plus more for serving

1 large handful chopped **fresh parsley**

2 tablespoons **Italian seasoning**

1 tablespoon **kosher salt**

2 teaspoons **garlic powder**

2 teaspoons **onion powder**

1 teaspoon **black pepper**

Cooking spray

1 cup (113g) **shredded mozzarella,** divided

Fresh basil leaves

1 Cook the spaghetti in boiling water according to package instructions. Drain, then mix half of the pasta with 1 cup (225g) marinara sauce.

2 Preheat the oven to 400°F (200°C) and line a large baking sheet with parchment paper.

3 To a large bowl, add the beef, breadcrumbs, eggs, milk, Parmesan, parsley, Italian seasoning, salt, garlic powder, onion powder, and black pepper. Mix to combine.

4 Line another large bowl with plastic wrap and lightly grease with cooking spray. Add the meatball mixture and press evenly around the bottom and edges of the bowl all the way to the top.

5 Sprinkle half of the mozzarella onto the bottom of the meatball mixture, then add the pasta with the marinara sauce. Top with the remaining mozzarella. Using the plastic wrap to guide you, create an enclosed meatball about ½-inch (1cm) thick, with the spaghetti in the center.

6 Carefully transfer the meatball to the baking sheet and bake for 50 to 60 minutes, until the meat is cooked through.

7 Serve over the remaining spaghetti and top with marinara sauce, more Parmesan, and basil.

CACIO E PEPE RISOTTO

Cacio e pepe means "cheese and pepper" in Italian. Usually, it's a perfect combo for pasta, but I love it in a gooey bowl of risotto. This is one of my favorite warm and cozy dinners!

4 cups (1L) **vegetable stock**

2 tablespoons **unsalted butter**

1 **shallot,** minced

2 **garlic cloves,** minced

Kosher salt

1 cup (220g) **arborio rice**

¼ cup (56g) **mascarpone** or **sour cream**

1 cup (100g) **grated Parmesan**

1 tablespoon **black pepper,** plus more for serving

1 Pour the vegetable stock into a medium saucepan and set over low heat to warm up. Adjust the heat as needed to maintain a gentle simmer.

2 In a large saucepan, melt the butter over medium heat. Add the shallot, garlic, and a generous pinch of salt. Stir occasionally with a wooden spoon until the shallot starts to soften, about 2 minutes. Add the rice and stir to coat in the butter. Cook the rice until the edges are just starting to turn translucent, about 2 minutes.

3 Reduce the heat to medium-low. Use a ladle to add enough stock to just cover the rice. Continue to stir the rice occasionally as the stock simmers. When it's almost completely absorbed, add more stock to cover and stir. Continue until all of the stock is added and the rice is tender, about 20 minutes total.

4 Reduce the heat to low and stir in the mascarpone. Add the Parmesan and black pepper and stir to combine. Let the mixture simmer until creamy and thick, about 2 more minutes. Taste for seasoning.

5 Use the ladle to divide the risotto between two bowls. Finish with more black pepper before serving.

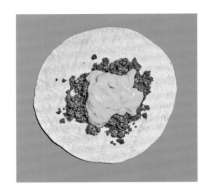
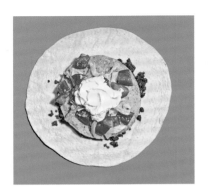

CRUNCHWRAPS
(MELLO'S VERSION)

This homemade version of the fast-food fave has all the crunchy, cheesy, meaty layers you love. It's shockingly easy to put together. Crank up the volume with some crushed chips for even more crunch!

2 tablespoons **vegetable oil,** divided

½ pound (227g) **ground beef or plant-based substitute**

2 teaspoons **chili powder** or **taco seasoning**

Kosher salt

Black pepper

2 large **flour tortillas**

2 tablespoons **cheese sauce**

2 **corn tostada shells**

¼ cup (57g) **sour cream**

½ cup (38g) **shredded lettuce**

¼ cup (25g) **chopped tomatoes**

½ cup (56g) **shredded cheddar**

½ cup (56g) **shredded Monterey Jack**

2 small **flour tortillas**

1 Heat 1 tablespoon of oil in a medium nonstick skillet over medium heat until it shimmers. Add the beef and cook, breaking it up with a wooden spoon, until no longer pink, about 3 minutes. Stir in the chili powder and a generous pinch of salt and black pepper. Continue cooking until the fat evaporates and the beef is browned, about 3 more minutes. Remove from the heat.

2 Lay the flour tortillas on a work surface. Divide the meat evenly between them, keeping it in the center of the tortillas. Spoon a tablespoon of cheese sauce over each, then set a tostada on top and gently press down. Spread the sour cream on top of each tostada, then evenly sprinkle the lettuce, tomato, and cheese over the top. Lay a small flour tortilla on top of each tostada.

3 Fold the edges of the large flour tortilla up toward the center, creating about 6 pleats so the tortilla wraps tightly around everything. Flip the tortilla so the folded side is down, then repeat with the second crunchwrap.

4 Heat the remaining 1 tablespoon of vegetable oil in the skillet over medium heat until it shimmers. Lay one of the tortillas, folded side down, in the skillet and cook until golden brown on the bottom, about 3 minutes. Flip and cook until golden brown on the other side, about 3 more minutes. Turn out onto a cutting board with the folded side down. Repeat with the second crunchwrap. Cut each one in half before serving.

✖✖ MELLO'S REMIX

Put the crunch in crunchwrap with some crushed-up Doritos, Ruffles, or Flamin' Hot Cheetos. Add a sprinkle over the meat and another one when you add the lettuce for a flavor explosion!

Break out the air fryer! *Once the tortillas are folded, coat both sides with nonstick spray. Place one in the basket and set the air fryer to 350°F (180°C) for 8 to 10 minutes, until the tortilla is golden brown. Repeat with the second crunchwrap.*

PHILLY CHEESESTEAK
(QUESADILLA REMIX)

Cheesesteaks and quesadillas are two of my favorite foods, so I combined them into one! Slices of steak, peppers, and onions get folded into a tortilla with plenty of cheese on the inside and even more cheese on the outside for dipping.

¼ pound (113g) **skirt steak**
Kosher salt
Black pepper
1 tablespoon **olive oil**
½ medium **white onion,** thinly sliced
½ **green bell pepper,** cut into strips
1 large **flour tortilla**
4 slices **provolone**
Chopped **fresh parsley**
Cheese sauce

1 Pat the steak dry with paper towels and season thoroughly on both sides with salt and black pepper.

2 Heat the oil in a large skillet over medium-high heat until it shimmers. Add the steak and cook until the bottom is charred, about 2 minutes. For medium-rare steak, flip and cook for 2 to 3 minutes more. (Cook 2 to 3 minutes more, flipping again, for well-done.) Transfer to a cutting board and tent with foil to rest.

3 Add the onion and bell pepper to the skillet and sauté until crisp-tender, stirring occasionally, for about 5 minutes. Remove to a plate. Slice the steak against the grain into thin strips.

4 Wipe out the skillet and set over medium heat. Center the tortilla in the skillet and lay two slices of cheese on top. Pile the steak and veggies on one side of the tortilla and lay the remaining two slices of cheese on top. Fold the tortilla in half over itself and cook until the bottom is nicely toasted, 3 minutes. Flip and cook until the cheese is melted, 3 more minutes.

5 Cut the quesadilla into four pieces. Serve with parsley sprinkled on top and cheese sauce for dipping.

☒☒ MELLO'S REMIX

When you're packing the meat and veggies on the tortilla, add a small pile of seasoned fries, crinkle fries, or waffle fries. Then layer on the cheese and continue as usual. It's a next level of delicious!

DINNER is SERVED. DIG IN!

ULTIMATE GRILLED CHEESE
(FEAT. KIMCHI)

Grilled cheese is the ultimate easy comfort food. But I'm always hungry for more! So I spiced things up with two of my favorite Korean condiments: kimchi for some briny crunch and gochujang for some heat. This is my ultimate grilled cheese.

3 tablespoons **mayonnaise**

1 tablespoon **gochujang**

2 slices **sandwich bread**

½ cup (55g) grated **white cheddar**

¼ cup (60g) **kimchi,** roughly chopped

1 Preheat a medium skillet over medium-low heat.

2 Whisk the mayonnaise and gochujang together in a small bowl. Slather both sides of each slice of bread with the mayo mixture.

3 Place one slice in the skillet, then pile on the cheese and kimchi, followed by the other slice. Gently press down with a spatula. Cook until the bottom is golden brown, about 6 minutes, then flip and cook until the cheese is gooey and melted, about 6 minutes more. Slice the grilled cheese in half before serving.

Break out the air fryer! *Line an air fryer basket with aluminum foil. Make the sandwich on top of the foil, then set the air fryer to 350°F (180°C) for 5 minutes. Flip and cook for another 5 minutes, until golden brown and melty.*

😈 MELLO'S REMIX

There's more than one way to grill a cheese! Swap out the kimchi for caramelized onions, a dollop of fig jam, crispy slices of bacon, sliced pickles, spinach and artichoke dip (page 53), some extra steak and peppers (page 102), or a smash burger patty (page 112).

PULL-APART CUBANO SLIDERS

These shortcut sliders have all my favorite flavors from the classic Cuban sandwich: slices of roast pork and ham, warm and melty Swiss cheese, plenty of mustard, and you can't forget the pickles! It's a bite of sandwich heaven.

Cooking spray

12 **pull-apart dinner rolls,** such as King's Hawaiian

½ cup (120g) **Dijon mustard**

12 **dill pickle slices**

8 ounces (227g) sliced **Swiss cheese**

8 ounces (227g) sliced **smoked ham**

8 ounces (227g) sliced **roast pork**

1 Preheat the oven to 400°F (200°C). Line a rimmed baking sheet with extra foil (to fold over the sandwich later) and spray well with cooking spray.

2 Keeping the rolls attached, slice laterally to create a group of top and bottom buns. Lay the halves on the prepared baking sheet, cut sides up.

3 Spread the mustard evenly over each half then place a pickle slice on each top bun. Layer the cheese over the pickles, then place the ham and pork slices on top. Place the bottom buns over the pork and wrap the entire thing with foil. (The sliders are upside down at this point, with the tops of the buns on the bottom.)

4 Bake for 10 minutes, then flip the foil package so the sliders are rightside up.

5 Bake for about 15 more minutes, until the cheese is fully melted. Remove to a cutting board and cut between each bun to make 12 sliders. Transfer to a platter and serve.

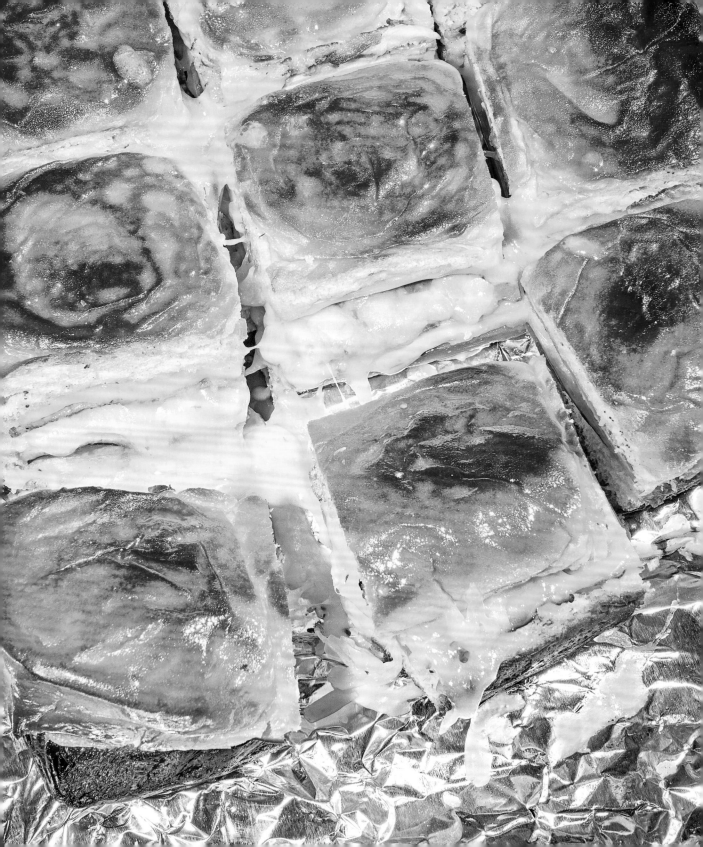

MEATBALL PARM SLIDERS
(FEAT. GARLIC BUNS)

These sliders are off the charts! The bread gets coated in butter and spices for a garlic knot flavor, then some gooey mozz and a saucy meatball get baked on top. It's a flavor explosion in every bite!

Cooking spray

12 **pull-apart dinner rolls,** such as King's Hawaiian

4 tablespoons **unsalted butter,** melted

1 teaspoon **garlic powder**

1 teaspoon **onion powder**

1 teaspoon **dried oregano**

½ teaspoon **red pepper flakes**

¼ cup (25g) grated **Parmesan**

1 pound (454g) **ground beef** or **plant-based substitute**

1 large **egg,** beaten

½ cup (50g) **panko breadcrumbs**

1 tablespoon **Italian seasoning**

Kosher salt

1 large ball **fresh mozzarella,** roughly torn

2 cups (226g) shredded **mozzarella**

1½ cups (337g) **marinara sauce**

Fresh basil

1. Preheat the oven to 350°F (180°C) and lightly grease a baking sheet with cooking spray. Line another baking sheet with aluminum foil.

2. Keeping the rolls attached, transfer to the greased baking sheet and carefully cut a hole into the top of each roll big enough to place in a golf-ball-sized meatball later on.

3. To a small bowl, add the butter, garlic powder, onion powder, oregano, and red pepper flakes. Mix to combine. Brush the insides and tops of the rolls with the mixture, then sprinkle all over with the Parmesan.

4. To a medium bowl, add the beef, egg, panko, Italian seasoning, and a big pinch of salt. Use clean hands to mix well and divide into 12 meatballs. Add a heaping tablespoon of fresh mozzarella to the center of each meatball, enclosing the cheese within the meat mixture to create a stuffed meatball. Transfer the meatballs to the lined baking sheet.

5. Place in the oven and cook for 10 to 12 minutes.

6. Using half of the shredded mozzarella, sprinkle each roll with cheese, then add a small spoonful of marinara sauce. Place a meatball into each hole (only the bottom of each meatball will sit in the hole), then top with more marinara sauce and the remaining mozzarella.

7. Place in the oven for 6 to 8 minutes, until the mozzarella starts to brown and bubble. Top with fresh basil and serve up!

SMASH BURGER SUPREME

Smash burgers are my favorite, because the flat patties mean more delicious, charred flavor. I like to go deluxe with cheese, all the toppings, and an army of condiments, but you do you! And for my Fortnite fans, I added an easy hack to make your Smash Burger into Durr Burger.

Vegetable oil
¼ pound (113g) **ground beef** or **plant-based substitute**
Kosher salt
Black pepper
1 slice **American cheese**
1 **hamburger bun,** toasted

FOR SERVING
Tomato
Onion
Lettuce
Ketchup
Mustard
Mayonnaise
Relish

1 Heat a medium nonstick skillet over medium-high heat for about 2 minutes. Brush with a thin layer of vegetable oil.

2 Pat the ground beef into a loose ball and set in the center of the skillet. Place a flat spatula over the meat and use the handle of a wooden spoon to slowly press down to flatten out the patty. Season with a pinch of salt and pepper and sear for about 2 minutes, until the edges are browned.

3 Flip the burger and set the slice of cheese on top. Cook for about 2 more minutes, until the cheese is melted and the burger is cooked through. Transfer to the bun and serve with your choice of toppings.

☽☾ MELLO'S REMIX

With a little dress-up, you can go from smash burger to Durr Burger, my favorite Fortnite bite. Cook a slice of turkey bacon (or any plant-based substitute) and drape it over the patty to make a tongue. Cut a pitted black olive in half and use a toothpick to skewer each one on a pearl onion, then stick the eyes on the burger bun. Slide a toothpick through a pimento olive and set it on top. Order up!

RAMEN CARBONARA
(FEAT. EGG & BACON)

A true Italian carbonara is made with pasta, but I'm all about creative cooking, so why not throw some ramen in the mix? The sauce is an easy mix of bacon, egg, and cheese for a rich and creamy sauce that takes almost no effort.

1 (3-ounce/85g) package **ramen noodles**

2 slices **bacon,** cut into ½-inch (1cm) pieces

2 tablespoons **unsalted butter**

1 large **egg,** beaten

½ cup (50g) **grated Parmesan,** plus more for serving

Kosher salt

Black pepper

1 Cook the ramen noodles according to the package directions. (Reserve the seasoning packet for another use.) Drain.

2 Meanwhile, add the bacon to a medium skillet and set over medium heat. Let the fat slowly render until the bacon is golden brown on the bottom, about 4 minutes. Flip and cook the other side until golden brown, about 2 more minutes. Remove the bacon to paper towels to drain, but leave the fat in the skillet.

3 With the skillet over medium heat, add the butter. As soon as the butter is melted, add the ramen and toss to coat. Pour over the egg and toss again until the noodles are glossy.

4 Sprinkle in the Parmesan, a pinch of salt, lots of black pepper, and the cooked bacon. Toss again to incorporate.

5 Transfer to a bowl and finish with a little more Parmesan and black pepper before serving.

"NUMB"ING NASI GORENG
(FEAT. CRISPY GARLIC EGG)

This Indonesian fried rice is one of my favorite recipes. I love the mix of sweet and spicy in the sauce. And just when I think my mouth is about to go numb, a crispy garlic egg comes to the rescue to balance things out!

2 tablespoons **vegetable oil,** divided

1 cup (175g) cooked **white rice,** preferably day-old

½ cup (70g) **frozen peas**

1 **scallion,** thinly sliced, plus more for serving

1 **red Thai chili** (or for more heat, a bird's eye chili), diced, plus more for serving

1 tablespoon **sweet soy sauce**

1 tablespoon **gochujang**

1 tablespoon **shrimp paste** (optional)

3 **garlic cloves,** thinly sliced

1 large **egg**

½ **avocado,** sliced

1 tablespoon **chili oil**

1 Heat one tablespoon of the vegetable oil in a wok or large skillet over high heat. Add the rice, peas, scallion, and chili, and stir-fry until the peas are thawed, about 2 minutes. Add the soy sauce, gochujang, and shrimp paste (if using) and continue stirring until the rice is coated and warmed through, about 2 more minutes. Transfer to a bowl.

2 Place a small nonstick skillet over medium heat and add the remaining oil. Add the garlic and cook until lightly golden, 1 to 2 minutes. Push the garlic to one side of the skillet and crack in the egg. Immediately add the garlic to the top of the egg and cook until the white is set, about 3 minutes. Place over the nasi goreng.

3 Top with avocado, chili oil, and extra scallion and chili.

☠ MELLO'S REMIX

Make your own sweet soy sauce by simmering ¼ cup (60ml) soy sauce (or tamari) and ¼ cup (53g) dark brown sugar over medium heat. When the mixture reduces into a syrupy consistency, pull it off the heat and cool completely. Store in a jar for up to 1 month.

TWICE-BAKED BUFFALO CHICKEN POTATOES

This is a baked potato like you've never had before! The soft and creamy potato gets filled with a spicy Buffalo chicken mixture and baked until it's warm, cheesy, and unbelievably delicious.

4 **large russet potatoes**
1 tablespoon **vegetable oil**
Kosher salt
2½ cups (350g) **shredded chicken breast**
½ cup (120ml) **Buffalo sauce**, plus more for serving
½ cup (55g) **shredded cheddar**, plus more for serving
⅓ cup (75g) **cream cheese**
1 **scallion,** finely chopped, plus more for serving
2 tablespoons **butter,** melted
2 tablespoons **ranch seasoning**
Black pepper

1 Preheat the oven to 425°F (220°C). Line a large baking sheet with parchment paper.

2 Use a fork to poke some holes in each potato, then rub each potato with oil and sprinkle with salt.

3 Place on the baking sheet and bake for about 1 hour, until fully cooked. Remove from the oven and let cool, about 15 minutes.

4 Cut each potato lengthwise down the middle, being careful not to cut all the way through. Using a spoon, scoop out the potato flesh and transfer to a medium bowl.

5 Add the chicken, Buffalo sauce, cheddar, cream cheese, scallion, butter, and ranch seasoning. Mix to combine.

6 Fill the hollowed-out potato skins with the Buffalo chicken filling and top each with more cheddar.

7 Lower the oven temperature to 350°F (180°C). Place the potatoes back in the oven for 15 to 20 minutes, until the filling is gooey and bubbling.

8 Top with more Buffalo sauce and scallions and enjoy!

"HAPPIER" HANDROLLS

Handrolls are a traditional style of sushi, rolled into a cone shape and meant to be eaten by hand. They're also an easy way to make a build-your-own spread so everyone can mix their perfect bite.

FOR THE RICE
1½ cups (270g) **sushi rice**
1 cup (240ml) **water,** plus more for rinsing
2 tablespoons **unseasoned rice vinegar**
1 tablespoon **sugar**
Kosher salt

FOR THE HANDROLLS
6 **nori sheets,** halved
Vegetables: **takuan** (pickled radish), **sprouts, carrot** matchsticks, **cucumber** matchsticks, **avocado** slices
Proteins: sashimi-grade **tuna, yellowtail,** or **uni; crab sticks; salmon roe** or **vegan caviar;** grilled **tofu,** cooked **shrimp**
Soy sauce
Wasabi paste

☒☒ MELLO'S REMIX

Get extra crunchy by using the shrimp from the Spicy Baja Shrimp Taco Bowls (page 93) as a filling.

1 **Make the rice:** In a medium bowl, cover the rice with plenty of cold water. Swirl the rice with your fingers to release the starch, then drain. Repeat the process about three more times, until the water is mostly clear. Fill the bowl with cold water again and soak the rice for 30 minutes, then drain.

2 In a rice cooker or medium saucepan, combine the rice and 1 cup (240ml) water. If using a rice cooker, use the sushi rice or white rice setting. If using a saucepan, bring to a boil over high heat. Cover, reduce the heat to low, and simmer until the rice is cooked through, 12 to 15 minutes. Remove from the heat and let steam, covered, for about 10 minutes, until the rice is tender and fluffy.

3 In a small bowl, whisk together the vinegar, sugar, and a big pinch of salt until the sugar is dissolved, then drizzle over the rice. Use a wooden spoon or rice paddle to quickly and evenly fold in the vinegar. (Don't mix too much or the rice will get sticky!) Let cool for about 30 minutes.

4 Set out a platter with the nori, veggies, and proteins, plus bowls of soy sauce and wasabi for dipping.

5 **Make the handrolls:** Take a sheet of nori in your left palm, shiny side down with the bottom left corner over your thumb. Spread a thin layer of rice over the section of nori in your palm. Arrange the veggies and proteins diagonally on the rice, pointing to the top left corner. Use your thumb to fold the bottom left corner over the fillings to create a cone shape. Keep rolling the cone to the other side of the nori, then use a piece of rice to glue the final edge to the roll.

TREAT YOURSELF

MELLO TREATS
(TURNED-UP REMIX)

Why have regular rice cereal treats when you can up your game with Mello Treats? Get creative with your cereal and toppings for a turned-up remix that everyone will love!

Cooking spray
3 tablespoons **unsalted butter**
1 (10-ounce/283g) bag
  mini marshmallows
6 cups (180g) **cereal of choice**
Toppings of choice
  (see Mello's Remix)

1. Coat an 8-inch (20cm) square baking pan with cooking spray.

2. Melt the butter in a large Dutch oven or pot over medium-low heat. Add the marshmallows and stir constantly until melted, about 3 minutes. Remove from the heat and stir in the cereal.

3. Coat a rubber spatula in cooking spray and scrape the cereal mixture into the baking pan. Press into an even layer, using more spray as needed. Add toppings while the mixture is still sticky, then let sit for 1 hour at room temperature before slicing into bars and serving.

⊠⊠ MELLO'S REMIX

Use these creative toppings for the most turned-up bar:

- *Melted chocolate*
- *Mini marshmallows*
- *Crushed freeze-dried fruit*
- *Salted peanuts*
- *Toasted coconut flakes*
- *Chocolate chips*
- *Chopped dried fruit*
- *Peanut butter chips*
- *Sprinkles or edible glitter*

RAINBOW POPCORN BALLS
(WITH SPARKLING SPRINKLES)

Instead of classic popcorn balls, turn up the volume with rainbow colors and plenty of sparkling sprinkles. Whether you're making these for the holidays or just a hang with friends, they're sure to grab all the attention!

1 tablespoon **unsalted butter**

1 (10-ounce/283g) bag
  mini marshmallows

Food coloring, any color

10 cups (50g) **popcorn**

Cooking spray

1 cup (170g) **white
  chocolate chips**

1 tablespoon **coconut oil**

Sparkling sugar sprinkles,
  any color

1 Melt the butter in a large Dutch oven or pot over medium-low heat. Add the marshmallows and stir constantly until melted, about 3 minutes.

2 Divide the marshmallow mixture evenly between medium bowls, using a separate bowl for each color you'd like to make. Add a few drops of food coloring to each bowl, creating a different color in each bowl, and use a spoon to stir into the marshmallow mixture. Divide the popcorn between bowls and use the same spoon to fold the popcorn and marshmallow mixture together.

3 Let the mixture cool for about 5 minutes. Line two rimmed baking sheets with parchment paper. Spray your hands with cooking spray, then grab about ½ cup (65g) of the mixture and roll into a ball. Repeat with the remaining mixture, then arrange the rolled balls on the baking sheets.

4 Add the chocolate chips and coconut oil to a small microwave-safe bowl. Microwave on high for about 1 minute, stopping to stir halfway, until melted. Stir to ensure the oil is fully incorporated.

5 Use a small spoon to drizzle the melted chocolate over the popcorn balls and finish with a pinch of sugar sprinkles. Let sit at room temperature for about 15 minutes, until the chocolate is set, then serve.

☺ MELLO'S REMIX

Get festive by dyeing the balls in holiday colors or adding M&Ms in holiday colors, crushed peppermint candies along with the popcorn, and sprinkles in creative shapes.

"RESCUE ME" ROCKY ROAD CLUSTERS

These easy rocky road bars use five ingredients and come together in a flash. Bet you can't eat just one!

Cooking spray
2 tablespoons **unsalted butter**
1 (14-ounce/397g) can **sweetened condensed milk**
1 (12-ounce/340g) bag **semisweet chocolate chips**
1 (16-ounce/453g) container **dry roasted peanuts**
1 (10-ounce/283g) bag **mini marshmallows**

1 Line a 9 x 13-inch (23 x 33cm) baking dish with parchment paper and coat with cooking spray.

2 Add the butter, condensed milk, and chocolate chips to a large Dutch oven or pot. Set over medium-low heat. Stir until the chocolate is melted, about 3 minutes. Remove from the heat and stir in the peanuts and marshmallows.

3 Coat a rubber spatula with cooking spray and scrape the mixture into the baking dish. Press into an even layer, using more cooking spray as needed. Refrigerate for 1 hour until set, then cut into squares.

CHOCOLATE MICE

Almost too cute to eat, these chocolate mice are easy on effort and big on creativity. Let your artistic side run wild with decorations, then chow down on your delicious creations!

7 **double-stuffed chocolate sandwich cookies,** such as Oreos

½ cup (85g) **semisweet chocolate chips**

8 sliced **almonds**

Candy eye decorations

Black licorice wheels

1 Add the cookies to a medium bowl. Use the handle of a wooden spoon to crush them into small pieces. Add the chocolate chips to a small microwave-safe bowl. Microwave on high for about 30 seconds, stopping to stir halfway, until melted.

2 Scrape the melted chocolate over the cookie crumbs and stir to combine. Refrigerate for about 30 minutes, until firm.

3 Scoop about 2 tablespoons of the chocolate mixture and use your hands to shape into a cylinder with a pointed tip. Flatten one of the long sides of the cylinder. Set on a plate.

4 Cut a sliced almond in half crosswise and insert each half on top of the pointed tip to make ears. Add candy decorations for eyes. Unroll the licorice and cut off a 3-inch (7.5cm) piece to make a tail. Repeat with the remaining chocolate mixture and decorations. Serve immediately or refrigerate in an airtight container for up to 24 hours.

EDIBLE COOKIE DOUGH
(NO-BAKE MIX)

The hardest part of making cookies is not eating the raw cookie dough. This recipe solves that problem with an entire batch of dough just for eating!

1 cup (120g) **all-purpose flour**
1 cup (213g) **dark brown sugar**
8 tablespoons **unsalted butter,** room temperature
1 tablespoon **heavy cream**
1 tablespoon **vanilla extract**
½ teaspoon **kosher salt**
½ cup (85g) **semisweet chocolate chips**

1 Add the flour to a small microwave-safe bowl. Microwave on high for about 2 minutes, stopping to stir every 30 seconds, until very hot and slightly toasted. Set aside to cool.

2 Add the brown sugar and butter to a medium bowl. Use a hand mixer on medium speed to beat together until light and fluffy, about 3 minutes. Add the heavy cream, vanilla, and salt and beat again until combined. Add the flour and chocolate chips and use a rubber spatula to fold until combined.

3 Cover the bowl with plastic wrap and refrigerate for 30 minutes, until the dough is firm. Scoop out 1-tablespoon portions and roll into balls. Arrange the balls evenly on a serving plate. Serve immediately or transfer to an airtight container and refrigerate for up to 1 week.

☺ MELLO'S REMIX

Swap the chocolate chips for:

- *¼ cup (38g) raisins, ¼ cup (23g) rolled oats, and ½ teaspoon ground cinnamon*
- *¼ cup (68g) peanut butter and ¼ cup (43g) peanut butter chips*
- *¼ cup (43g) white chocolate chips and 2 tablespoons hot fudge*
- *¼ cup (48g) rainbow sprinkles*
- *¼ cup (13g) crushed mini pretzels and ¼ cup (7g) crushed potato chips*

TOASTED MARSHMELLO S'MORES PIE
(FEAT. STUFFED PUFFS)

I had to include s'mores in my book, and you know I'm always going to go big! This s'mores pie has a graham cracker crust, a brownie filling, and toasted marshmallows on top—in other words, it's my masterpiece!

FOR THE CRUST

12 **graham crackers,** crushed

¼ cup (50g) **sugar**

4 tablespoons **unsalted butter,** melted

FOR THE PIE

8 tablespoons **unsalted butter,** melted

1 cup (200g) **sugar**

2 large **eggs**

Kosher salt

½ cup (60g) **all-purpose flour**

½ cup (42g) **cocoa powder**

Stuffed marshmallows, such as Stuffed Puffs, halved widthwise

1 Preheat the oven to 350°F (180°C).

2 **Make the crust:** In a large bowl, whisk the graham cracker crumbs and sugar together. Add the butter and use a rubber spatula to stir until hydrated. Pour into a 9-inch (23cm) pie plate and press into an even layer along the bottom and up the sides.

3 **Make the pie:** In the same large bowl, whisk the butter and sugar together. Add the eggs one at a time and whisk to combine. Add a big pinch of salt, then add the flour and cocoa powder. Use a rubber spatula to stir into a thick batter. Scrape the batter into the crust and smooth into an even layer.

4 Bake for about 30 minutes, until a toothpick inserted into the center comes out clean. Remove the pie from the oven.

5 Increase the temperature to 500°F (260°C). Arrange the marshmallow halves around the surface of the pie. Return to the oven for about 5 minutes, checking every minute or so, until the marshmallows are toasted. Let cool for about 10 minutes before slicing and serving.

AIR-FRIED OREOS

The classic carnival snack gets the air fryer treatment—no mess and just as delicious. An easy batter cooks until it's crunchy on the outside with a warm Oreo at the center. It doesn't get better than this!

Cooking spray
1 large **egg**
¼ cup (60ml) **whole milk**
1 teaspoon **vanilla extract**
1 cup (120g) **all-purpose flour**
2 tablespoons **sugar**
2 teaspoons **baking powder**
Kosher salt
8 **chocolate sandwich cookies,**
  such as Oreos
Confectioners' sugar

1. Line an air fryer basket with aluminum foil and coat with cooking spray.

2. In a large bowl, whisk the egg, milk, and vanilla together. Add the flour, sugar, baking powder, and a big pinch of salt and whisk to form a very thick, cakelike batter.

3. Add 4 of the cookies to the batter and use a fork to flip and fully coat with batter. Transfer the cookies to the air fryer basket and coat the tops with cooking spray.

4. Set the fryer to 350°F (180°C) for about 7 minutes, until the cookies are golden brown. Transfer the cookies to a plate. Batter and fry the remaining 4 cookies. Dust with confectioners' sugar before serving.

No air fryer? *Deep-fry these instead! Heat 1 quart (1L) of vegetable oil in a Dutch oven to 350°F (180°C). Working in batches, fry the battered Oreos until golden brown, flipping halfway, about 2 minutes. Use tongs to transfer to paper towels to drain. Continue frying in batches, adjusting the heat to make sure the oil stays at a steady temperature.*

☺ MELLO'S REMIX

Set out ice cream in any flavor to soften for about 5 minutes. Place a small scoop of ice cream on top of a fried Oreo, then gently press another fried Oreo on top. Continue scooping and making ice cream sandwiches, then arrange on a plate and freeze for 30 minutes, until firm.

"FAIRYTALE" FRIED ICE CREAM

Just like a fairy tale, this "fried" ice cream is too good to be true. Instead of a messy deep fry, these balls of ice cream get rolled in crushed cereal for the same crunchy outside. You and your dessert will live happily ever after!

4 tablespoons **unsalted butter**

3 cups (84g) **puffed rice cereal,** such as Rice Krispies, crushed

1 teaspoon **ground cinnamon**

2 pints (650g) **ice cream,** any flavor

TOPPINGS (OPTIONAL)

Caramel sauce

Rainbow sprinkles

Toasted sesame seeds

Honey

Crushed freeze-dried **fruit**

Chocolate drizzle

Cinnamon sugar

Chopped **nuts**

Whipped cream

1 Melt the butter in a large skillet over medium heat. Add the crushed cereal and cinnamon and toss to coat. Toast the cereal, stirring often, until golden brown, about 5 minutes. Pour the mixture into a large shallow bowl and cool completely, about 30 minutes.

2 Scoop the ice cream into four large balls. (Use your hands to form the scoops into perfect balls, but work quickly so they don't melt too much!) Roll the balls in the cereal mixture, gently pressing to adhere on all sides. Set on a large plate and freeze for at least 15 minutes, until firm, or up to 24 hours in advance. Serve with your favorite toppings.

"CANDY KID" CAKE POPS

These cake pops use an easy hack—donut holes—for a fast and delicious treat. They're the perfect blank canvas to get creative and let your inner candy kid run wild!

1 (12-ounce/340g) bag
   white chocolate chips
1 tablespoon **coconut oil**
Food coloring, any color
24 **donut holes,** any flavor
Candy decorations

SPECIAL EQUIPMENT
Cardboard box
Wooden skewers

1   Add the chocolate chips and coconut oil to a medium microwave-safe bowl. Microwave on high for about 90 seconds, stopping to stir every 30 seconds, until melted. Stir to ensure the oil is fully incorporated.

2   Keep the mixture in a single bowl for a white cake pop, or divide the mixture into separate bowls and add a few drops of food coloring to each one to make as many different colors as you want.

3   Poke small holes in a cardboard box to dry the cake pops. Dip the tip of a skewer into the chocolate, then skewer a donut hole. Dip the donut into the chocolate, letting the excess fully drip off, before setting the skewer upright in the box.

4   Let the chocolate set for about 5 minutes before adding any candy decorations, then return to the box to fully set, about 1 hour. Serve immediately or refrigerate for up to 3 days.

☭☭ MELLO'S REMIX

Literally, make a mini Marshmello! Dip a stuffed marshmallow in the melted white chocolate mixture, then chill until fully set, about 1 hour. Use black gel icing to pipe two Xs for eyes and a mouth. Chill again for about 30 minutes to set the icing.

CRAVING DESSERT FIRST? TREAT YOURSELF!

FROZEN BANANA POPS
(FEAT. RAINBOW CEREAL)

An easy treat for hot days, these frozen bananas get dipped in chocolate and covered in crunchy cereal. They're sweet, satisfying, and simple to make!

4 large **bananas,** slightly firm

1 (12-ounce/340g) bag **semisweet chocolate chips**

1 tablespoon **coconut oil**

2 cups (120g) **colorful cereal,** such as Fruity Pebbles

Edible glitter (optional)

SPECIAL EQUIPMENT
Wooden skewers

1 Line a rimmed baking sheet with parchment paper.

2 Peel the bananas and cut in half crosswise. Skewer and set on the baking sheet. Cover with plastic wrap and freeze until solid, about 3 hours.

3 When the bananas are frozen, add the chocolate chips and coconut oil to a medium microwave-safe bowl. Microwave on high for about 90 seconds, stopping to stir every 30 seconds, until melted. Stir to incorporate the oil, then pour the mixture into a tall glass. Pour the cereal onto a plate and spread out evenly.

4 Dip the frozen bananas in the chocolate, then let the excess fully drip off before rolling in the cereal. Return to the baking sheet and sprinkle with edible glitter, if using. Continue dipping and rolling the remaining bananas. Serve immediately or wrap in plastic and freeze for up to 3 days.

CHOCOLATE CHIP SKILLET COOKIE
(À LA MODE MIX)

Chocolate chip cookies are always perfect, but when they're skillet-sized, warm, and served with ice cream, they're even better. Stick with a classic cookie or stir in your favorite add-ins for your dream dessert!

Cooking spray

1 stick (113g) **unsalted butter,** room temperature

1 cup (213g) packed **light brown sugar**

½ cup (110g) **granulated sugar**

2 teaspoons **pure vanilla extract**

1 large **egg**

1½ cups (180g) **all-purpose flour**

¾ teaspoon **baking soda**

½ teaspoon **kosher salt**

1 (12-ounce/340g) bag **semisweet chocolate chips,** divided

Vanilla ice cream

Caramel sauce

Hot fudge

1 Preheat the oven to 350°F (180°C). Thoroughly coat a 10-inch (25cm) cast-iron skillet with cooking spray.

2 To a large bowl, add the butter, brown sugar, granulated sugar, and vanilla extract. Use a handheld mixer to beat until the sugar is incorporated and the butter is fluffy, about 4 minutes. Add the egg and beat again to incorporate.

3 Add the flour, baking soda, and salt. Use a rubber spatula to fold in until almost incorporated. Reserve ½ cup (85g) of the chocolate chips, then pour the rest of the bag into the bowl. Continue folding until completely combined.

4 Transfer the cookie dough to the skillet and smooth to the edges in an even layer. Top with the reserved chocolate chips. Bake for 20 to 25 minutes, until the edges are golden brown and the center is set but still a little gooey.

5 Serve directly from the skillet with scoops of ice cream and drizzles of caramel and hot fudge.

☒☒ MELLO'S REMIX

Before baking, stir in M&Ms, crushed pretzels, coconut flakes, salted peanuts, chopped nuts, or any other favorite cookie add-ins.

FUNFETTI CELEBRATION MUG CAKE

When you're baking for one, a mug cake is the way to go! Everything gets mixed and microwaved all in one mug, plus it's ready in a matter of seconds. Working smarter not harder is always worth a celebration!

Cooking spray

3 tablespoons **all-purpose flour**

2 tablespoons **sugar**

¼ teaspoon **baking powder**

Kosher salt

2 tablespoons **unsalted butter,** melted

1 tablespoon **whole milk**

1 large **egg**

1 teaspoon **vanilla extract**

1 tablespoon **rainbow confetti sprinkles**

1 Coat a microwave-safe mug with cooking spray. Add the flour, sugar, baking powder, and a big pinch of salt. Use a fork to whisk until combined.

2 Add the butter, milk, egg, vanilla, and sprinkles and whisk again, making sure to scrape along the bottom.

3 Microwave on high for 60 seconds, until the top of the cake is fully set. (Microwave in additional 10-second intervals as needed.) Serve immediately.

Break out the air fryer!
Skip the microwave and set the air fryer to 350°F (180°C) for 10 minutes.

GIANT MOLTEN LAVA CAKE

This easy Bundt cake gets a molten lava center of gooey chocolate ganache. It's an impressive cake for serving a crowd!

Cooking spray
1 (15.25-ounce/432g) box **chocolate cake mix**
1¼ cups (300ml) **water**
½ cup (120ml) **vegetable oil**
3 large **eggs**
16 ounces (454g) **dark chocolate,** chopped
2 cups (480ml) **heavy cream**
Cocoa powder, for serving

1 Preheat the oven to 350°F (180°C). Coat a 10-inch (25cm) Bundt pan with cooking spray.

2 In a large bowl, mix the cake mix, water, oil, and eggs to form a smooth batter. Pour into the Bundt pan.

3 Bake for 35 to 45 minutes, until a toothpick inserted in the center comes out clean. Let cool in the pan.

4 Add the chocolate to a medium bowl. Add the heavy cream to a small saucepan and set over medium-high heat. Heat for 2 to 3 minutes, until the cream starts to simmer. Pour the cream over the chocolate and let sit for 2 minutes. Whisk until the chocolate has melted and the mixture is smooth.

5 Set a large serving plate over the Bundt pan and flip to release the cake. Pour the chocolate mixture into the center of the cake. Dust the cake all over with cocoa powder before serving with the remaining chocolate sauce for drizzling.

CEREAL MILK ICE CREAM

Let's be honest: The best part of a bowl of cereal is drinking the milk at the end. This easy ice cream soaks up all that good cereal flavor for a delicious breakfast for dessert!

2 cups (120g) **cereal of choice,** divided

2 cups (480ml) **heavy cream,** cold

1 (14-ounce/397g) can **sweetened condensed milk**

1 Mix 1 cup (60g) cereal and the heavy cream in a large bowl. Set in the refrigerator to soak and let the flavors infuse for 15 minutes. Use a slotted spoon or small strainer to scoop out the cereal (it's fine if some is left behind).

2 Use a hand mixer to beat the cream into soft peaks, about 3 minutes. Add the sweetened condensed milk and beat again to form stiff peaks, about 2 more minutes. Add the remaining 1 cup (60g) cereal and fold to combine.

3 Scrape the mixture into an 8-inch (20cm) square baking pan. Cover tightly with plastic wrap and freeze for about 4 hours, until firm, or up to 1 week. Let sit at room temperature for a few minutes before scooping.

CINNAMON-RAISIN MONKEY BREAD
(FEAT. GOOEY VIBES)

Monkey bread is like a cinnamon roll, but on a giant scale. And it's so easy to pull apart into bites. This monkey bread is extra gooey to make sure every bite is warm and delicious.

Cooking spray

½ cup (100g) **granulated sugar**

1 teaspoon **ground cinnamon**

½ cup (85g) **raisins**

½ cup (57g) **chopped walnuts**

2 (16.3-ounce/462g) cans **jumbo biscuits,** such as Pillsbury Grands, or 2 pounds (907g) pizza dough

8 tablespoons **unsalted butter,** melted

1 cup (213g) **dark brown sugar**

1 Preheat the oven to 350°F (180°C). Coat a 10-inch (25cm) Bundt pan with cooking spray. Set the pan on a rimmed baking sheet.

2 In a large bowl, whisk together the granulated sugar and cinnamon. Add the raisins and walnuts and toss to coat.

3 Separate the biscuits and cut each one into quarters. Add the biscuit pieces to the sugar mixture and toss to coat. Sprinkle the biscuit pieces, raisins, walnuts, and any remaining sugar mixture around the Bundt pan as evenly as possible.

4 In a medium microwave-safe bowl, melt the butter on high for 30 to 60 seconds. Add the brown sugar and whisk until combined. Pour the mixture evenly over the dough in the pan.

5 Bake for about 30 minutes, until puffed and golden brown. Cool in the pan for 5 minutes, then set a large serving plate on top of the pan and quickly flip to release the monkey bread and sugar syrup. Serve immediately.

GLASS HALF FULL

SLURP JUICE

When I'm feeling knocked down, a little slurp juice boosts my health. This recipe is a copy of the Fortnite drink, with two colors magically floating in the same glass. Slurp away!

Ice

Green and blue food coloring (optional)

1 cup (240ml) **green sports drink,** such as Powerade

1 cup (240ml) **blue sugar-free sports drink,** such as Powerade

1 Fill a tall glass with ice.

2 If desired, add a drop of green food coloring to the green drink and a drop of blue food coloring to the blue drink to intensify the colors.

3 Add the green drink to the jar. Turn a spoon upside down and hold it diagonally into the jar so it's touching the side. Slowly pour the blue drink over the back of a spoon so it floats on top of the green. Serve immediately.

NOTE: *It's important to use one regular and one sugar-free drink, because the sugar-free drink is slightly lighter and will float. Two of the same type of drink will mix together, and you'll end up with a glass of bummer juice.*

SHIELD POTION BUBBLE TEA

Level up with this boba inspired by my favorite game, Fortnite. I like using crystal boba for an authentic look, but any type of boba will increase your shield points!

1 cup (240ml) **water**
¼ cup (50g) **sugar**
1 **butterfly pea tea bag** or
   1 teaspoon **butterfly pea tea**
½ cup (90g) precooked **crystal boba** or ¼ cup (40g) **dried crystal boba**
Ice

SPECIAL EQUIPMENT
Cocktail shaker
Boba straw

1 In a small saucepan, bring the water to a boil. Remove from the heat and whisk in the sugar.

2 Add the tea bag and steep for about 10 minutes, until the water is deep blue. Discard the tea bag. If using loose tea, add it directly to the saucepan, then strain the liquid after steeping.

3 Rinse and drain the precooked boba, or boil the dried boba according to the package directions and drain well. Add to a glass.

4 Fill a cocktail shaker with plenty of ice, then add the tea. Shake until the outside is frosty, then strain into the glass over the boba. Serve immediately with a boba straw.

"SPOTLIGHT" GRAPE SODA

This homemade grape soda can be a fun project (made with fresh grapes) or an easy hack (made with grape jelly). Either way you make it, it's a drink that will steal the spotlight.

FOR THE SYRUP
1 bunch **Concord grapes,** about 1 pound (454g), removed from the stem
½ cup (100g) **sugar**
½ cup (120ml) **water**

FOR THE SODA
Ice
Plain seltzer or **club soda**

1 **Make the syrup:** To a medium saucepan, add the grapes, sugar, and water. Bring to a boil over medium heat, then reduce the heat to low and simmer for about 30 minutes, until the grapes are extremely soft.

2 Remove from the heat and use a wooden spoon to smash the grapes. Strain through a fine mesh strainer into an airtight container and refrigerate for at least 2 hours or until ready to use. (The syrup will keep in the refrigerator for up to 3 weeks.)

3 **Make the soda:** Fill glasses with ice and add ½ cup (120ml) of grape syrup. Top with seltzer and serve.

Can't find Concord grapes? Grab a jelly jar instead! Add 1 cup (340g) grape jelly, ½ cup (100g) sugar, and ½ cup (120ml) water to a medium saucepan. Set over low heat and whisk until the sugar and jelly are totally combined, about 2 minutes.

☠ MELLO'S REMIX

The only thing more refreshing than a cold grape soda is a cold grape soda over frozen grapes. Throw some loose grapes in an airtight container and freeze overnight for a deliciously edible ice cube!

PIÑA WHIP

Frosty, delicious, and simple to make, this piña whip is packed with pineapple and coconut. No matter where you are, you'll hear the ocean waves and feel the tropical breeze!

2 cups (340g) **frozen pineapple pieces**
½ cup (120ml) **pineapple juice**
½ cup (120ml) **cream of coconut**
Juice of 1 **lime**
Maraschino cherries

1 Add the pineapple pieces, pineapple juice, cream of coconut, and lime juice to a blender. Blend on high until combined, 30 seconds to 1 minute, stopping to push the pineapple pieces down as needed.

2 Transfer to an airtight container and freeze for 30 minutes, until firm but not fully frozen.

3 Scoop into glasses or transfer to a ziplock bag, snip the corner off, and pipe into the glasses in swirls. Finish with a maraschino cherry on top!

PREP: 10 MINUTES **COOK:** 4 MINUTES **SERVES:** 2

"HITTA" HOT CHOCOLATE
(FEAT. STUFFED PUFFS)

Nothing says warm and cozy like hot chocolate—and marshmallows on top are always required. I love to add a few big Stuffed Puffs, but mini marshmallows are totally delicious, too.

FOR THE HOT CHOCOLATE
1 cup (240ml) **milk of choice**
½ cup (70g) **hot fudge topping**
2 tablespoons **heavy cream** or **coconut cream**
1 teaspoon **pure vanilla extract**

FOR THE GLASSES
¼ cup (35g) **hot fudge topping**
Crushed graham crackers
Stuffed marshmallows, such as Stuffed Puffs, any flavor

1 **Make the hot chocolate:** Add the milk and hot fudge to a small saucepan. Set over low heat and whisk until combined and warm, about 3 minutes. Remove from the heat and whisk in the heavy cream and vanilla.

2 **Assemble the glasses:** Spread the hot fudge on a small plate and spread the graham crackers on a separate small plate. Dip the rims of two martini glasses in the fudge, then twirl in the graham crackers. Divide the hot chocolate between the glasses.

3 Use tongs to hold a marshmallow over a gas burner or the flame of a lighter until the marshmallow flames and chars, about 30 seconds. Blow out the flame and set the marshmallow in a glass. Repeat with additional marshmallows as desired and serve.

MELLO'S REMIX

Instead of vanilla, add a pump or two of your favorite flavored syrup, like amaretto, peppermint, salted caramel, or toasted marshmallow, or a pinch of cayenne pepper for a spicy twist. A shot of espresso is also a perfect addition for a perky kick.

ULTIMATE GREEN SMOOTHIE
(THE MELLO MIXTAPE)

I love to start the day off right with a green smoothie. But healthy can still be delicious, and this formula lets you customize with all your favorite things. Get in there and mix it up!

1 cup (240ml) **milk of choice**
2 cups (about 135g) **greens**
1 cup (about 130g) **diced fruit**
2 tablespoons **nut butter**
1 tablespoon **sweetener**
Add-ins

1 Order matters for a smooth blend! To a large blender, add the milk first, followed by the greens, fruit, nut butter, sweetener, and add-ins.

2 Start blending on low and slowly increase speed to high until smooth, about 1 minute. Serve in glasses or portable drink containers on the go.

MILK	GREENS	FRUIT
Almond	Celery	Banana
Coconut	Kale	Berries
Dairy	Microgreens	Cherries
Oat	Spinach	Mango
Soy	Swiss chard	Pineapple

NUT BUTTER	SWEETENER	ADD-INS
Almond	Agave	Chia
Cashew	Date syrup	Coconut oil
Peanut	Honey	Collagen powder
Sunflower	Maple syrup	Flaxseed
Tahini	Stevia	Superfood powder

"BACK IT UP" BRAZILIAN LEMONADE SLUSHIES

Don't get it twisted: Even though it's called lemonade, this traditional Brazilian drink is made with whole limes for an extra tart and tangy drink. A quick zap in the blender with sweetened condensed milk and plenty of ice makes for a frosty and refreshing slushie.

4 cups (1L) **water,** divided
4 **limes,** quartered
1 (14 ounce/397g) can **sweetened condensed milk**

1 To a blender, add 2 cups (480ml) water and the limes (peels included!). Blend on high until the limes are totally broken down, 15 to 30 seconds. Blending too long will make the limes bitter, so keep it brief.

2 Set a fine mesh strainer over a pitcher and strain the juice, using a rubber spatula to help move the pulp as needed. Discard the pulp.

3 Stir in the condensed milk and the remaining 2 cups (480ml) of water. Serve immediately or refrigerate for up to 24 hours, stirring well before serving.

PREP: 5 MINUTES **COOK:** NONE **SERVES:** 1

ITALIAN CREAM SODA

A mix of syrup, seltzer, and cream might sound weird on paper, but together they're a surprisingly delicious drink! I like to sweeten the deal with a colorful rim.

Ice
¼ cup (60ml) **flavored fruit syrup,** such as Torani
Plain seltzer or **club soda**
2 tablespoons **heavy cream**

1. Fill a small glass with ice, then pour in the fruit syrup.
2. Fill the glass with seltzer, leaving a little room at the top, then drizzle in the cream. Stir before drinking.

MELLO'S REMIX

Dip the rim of the glass in melted white chocolate, then dip in a plate of colorful sanding sugar or Pop Rocks for an extra sweet soda.

"FEEL SOMETHING" FAUX-JITO

This herby, sweet, and bubbly drink will definitely make you feel something! A big burst of mint in every sip is the definition of cool and refreshing on a hot day.

6 **fresh mint leaves**
½ **lime,** cut into two wedges
Ice
1 (7.5 ounce/222ml) can **lemon-lime soda,** such as Sprite

1 Add the mint leaves and lime wedges to a Collins glass or tall glass. Use a muddler or the handle of a wooden spoon to lightly mash until the limes are juiced and the mint leaves are slightly broken up.

2 Pack the glass with ice and top with the soda. Use a straw to gently stir and enjoy.

FRUITY AGUA FRESCA
(ANY FRUIT REMIX)

Agua fresca is a traditional Mexican drink made from fresh fruit, usually sold in a variety of flavors. This recipe is the blueprint, so you can remix with whatever fruit you're craving the most, over and over again.

3 cups (720ml) **very cold water,** divided

4 cups (about 500g) **peeled and sliced fruit,** such as watermelon, pineapple, cantaloupe, cucumber, guanabana, or papaya

2 tablespoons **sugar,** plus more as needed

Juice of 1 **lime**

Ice

1 Add 1 cup (240ml) water to a blender, along with the fruit, sugar, and lime juice. Blend on high until smooth, about 1 minute. Set a fine mesh strainer over a pitcher and strain the juice, using a rubber spatula to help move the pulp as needed. Discard the pulp.

2 Stir the remaining 2 cups (480ml) of water into the pitcher. Taste and add more sugar or water as needed for the perfect balance.

3 Fill glasses with ice before serving.

☻☻ MELLO'S REMIX

Dip the rim of the glass in chamoy and Tajín for a tangy touch. And throw a tamarind straw in there to take it to the next level of delicious!

MANGO-"ESTI"-LASSI

When the temperatures rise in India, a mango lassi really cools things down. Fresh fruit and yogurt get blended with plenty of ice for a cold and delicious drink.

¼ cup (60ml) **milk of choice,** plus more as needed

1 cup (227g) **plain yogurt of choice** (not Greek-style yogurt)

1 cup (165g) **diced fresh mango** or **frozen mango**

2 tablespoons **sugar**

Pinch of **ground cardamom**

1 Order matters for a smooth blend! To a large blender, add the milk first, followed by the yogurt, mango, sugar, and cardamom.

2 Blend on high until smooth, about 1 minute, adding a splash more milk if needed. Pour into glasses and serve.

ICE CREAM FLOAT
(FEAT. FOUR FLAVORS)

The classic ice cream float gets reinvented in four of my favorite flavors, using strawberry soda, orange soda, sparkling apple cider, and kombucha. Serve them straight up or get creative with the toppings for the full experience!

2 scoops **vanilla ice cream**
Soda of choice
Whipped cream
Garnish of choice

Add the ice cream to a pint glass. Slowly pour over the soda, letting some of the foam settle before topping it off. Add a swirl of whipped cream and garnish before serving.

STRAWBERRY FIELDS

Use strawberry soda, such as Jarritos, and a red licorice straw to garnish.

DREAMSICLE

Use orange soda and orange jelly fruit slices to garnish.

APPLE OF MY PIE

Use sparkling apple cider and a drizzle of salted caramel to garnish.

POPPIN' BOOCH

Use kombucha and popping candy, such as Pop Rocks, to garnish.

☠ MELLO'S REMIX

A pinch of edible luster dust sends these floats to the top of the charts. Put it in the glass with the ice cream and watch it swirl as the soda pours over.

MATCHA BUBBLE TEA

When I'm a grumpy Mello, I usually need caffeine and a snack. This checks off both at once with an iced matcha latte loaded with the chewy deliciousness of boba. After just a few sips, I'm a happy Mello!

FOR THE BOBA
4 cups (1L) **water**
1 cup (152g) **black tapioca pearls**

FOR THE SYRUP
¼ cup (60ml) **water**
¼ cup (54g) packed
  dark brown sugar

FOR THE MATCHA
2 teaspoons **matcha powder**
½ cup (120ml) **water**
Ice
1 cup (240ml) **milk of choice**

SPECIAL EQUIPMENT
Boba straw

1 **Make the boba:** In a medium saucepan, bring the water to a boil over high heat. Add the tapioca pearls and cook according to package directions. Drain and set aside.

2 **Make the syrup:** Add the water and brown sugar to the same saucepan and set over medium heat. Whisk until all the sugar is dissolved and the mixture starts to simmer. Stir in the drained boba and remove from the heat.

3 **Make the matcha:** Add the matcha and water to a jar with a tight lid and shake until combined and frothy. (This can also be done in a glass with a mini frother.)

4 Divide the boba between two glasses, then fill with ice. Slowly pour ½ cup (120ml) milk into each glass to layer on top of the boba. Then slowly pour ¼ cup (60ml) matcha into each glass to layer on top of the milk. Serve immediately with a boba straw.

STRAWBERRY HORCHATA MILKSHAKE

Classic horchata, a Mexican rice drink, gets a sweet boost from fresh strawberries and a little ice cream for a thick milkshake texture. Yum!

½ cup (100g) **long-grain white rice,** rinsed and drained

½ cup (45g) **sliced almonds**

2 **cinnamon sticks**

1 cup (240ml) **boiling water**

1 pint (325g) **vanilla ice cream** (dairy or vegan)

1 pound (454g) **strawberries,** hulled and roughly chopped

1 Add the rice, almonds, and cinnamon sticks to a small bowl. Pour the boiling water over top and let sit for about 1 hour, until the mixture is cooled and the rice is soft.

2 Pour the entire contents of the bowl (including the liquid) into a blender and blend on high until smooth, about 2 minutes. Add the ice cream in scoops and the strawberries.

3 Blend on high again to form a mostly smooth mixture, about 30 seconds. Pour into two milkshake glasses and serve immediately.

ICED MASALA CHAI
(FEAT. COLD FOAM)

Sweet and spicy chai gets a delicious glow up, served over ice with a creamy cold foam on top. This recipe makes enough for two drinks, but you can make it a triple batch to enjoy all week!

FOR THE TEA

3 cups (720ml) **water**

½-inch (1cm) piece of **fresh ginger,** smashed

2 **green cardamom pods,** smashed

4 **whole cloves**

2 **black tea bags**

½ cup (120ml) **milk of choice**

2 teaspoons **sugar**

FOR THE FOAM

½ cup (120ml) **milk of choice**

1 tablespoon **confectioners' sugar**

1 **Make the tea:** To a small saucepan, add the water, ginger, cardamom, and cloves and bring to a boil over high heat.

2 Remove from the heat and add the tea bags. Steep for about 5 minutes, then discard the tea bags. Whisk in the milk and sugar and let the spices continue to steep until the mixture is cooled, about 30 minutes.

3 Using a fine mesh sieve to strain out the spices, pour the tea into a quart jar or airtight container. Refrigerate until ready to use or for up to 3 days.

4 **Make the foam:** Combine the milk and sugar. This can be made in a large glass with a mini frother, shaken in a pint glass with a tight lid, or added to a clean French press, moving the plunger up and down to froth. Mix until airy and doubled in size.

5 Fill two large glasses with ice. Divide the tea between the glasses and spoon the cold foam over top to float. Serve immediately.

INDEX

PUBLISHER'S ACKNOWLEDGMENTS

DK would like to thank everyone at the Shalizi Group for their role in bringing this book together. Thanks also to Noah Fecks and the entire food photography team: Susan Ottaviano, Ethan Lunkenheimer, Justin Skrakowski, Ben Weiner, Lizzie Rosin, and Liaden Leonard.